I0456218

The Cabin

at Girly Creek

Donna G. Hendricks

ISBN:1547216344
ISBN-13:9781547216345

Introduction

When I met my husband, John, for the first time, he was driving a little brown Toyota with a 17 foot shiny canoe draped over the top, like a silver fish swallowing a bug. He bought us each a muffin and coffee at McDonalds, saying he couldn't stay very long because he always listened to a radio program, and it would start soon. We sat down and talked for a little while.

"I've always wanted to build a get-away cabin," I said. He looked stunned.

"Me too," he said.

We drew cabin plans on a napkin, where the chicken house would be, and where the garden would be. Two and a half hours later, we finally parted.

The next time we met, he held an armload of books about cabins that he loaned me.

A couple of months later, we were married, looking for a woods, and collecting lumber and windows.

This is a true story, taken right out of my memory and journals.

Red Tailed Hawk

Acknowledgments

My husband, John, is the man who has led us to so many adventures. Without him, I probably would have been a couch potato and not writing books. I would also like to thank him for standing by me in my writing endeavors.

My daughter, Shirley, who has always been a great part of my life!

My stepson, Benjamin, who enriched and added so much to this adventure. He loved it all!

My stepdaughter, Jessica, who was willing to help out at the cabin.

Our friends and other relatives, who contributed their interest in our adventure, who gave us items with which to build, things to furnish the cabin, time, friendship, and so much more.

Whitetail Deer

Foreword

This book is the bringing together of nearly 20 years we spent on this cabin: finding the property, exploring, collecting supplies, planning, building, furnishing, and enjoying the fruits of our labor. Since a lot of years have passed, I referred to my journal, but I hadn't written down every detail. Sometimes I forgot to write in it, so I looked at photos we shot along the way to jog my memory. Also I found a map I drew many years ago of the layout of The Land, writing down all the names we gave places. If I couldn't recall details, I asked John to help me remember; so we brought a lot of it back by piecing it together again.

There were so many people involved with our cabin, I decided to cut down the number of names so it wouldn't be so confusing. For example, I might say: we took John's cousin for a hike down Girly Creek instead of using his/her name, but they know who they are. There was a lot of involvement with our neighbors. Since I didn't want to divulge personal information about anyone, I used fictional names for these real people. I used our names, plus the first names or nicknames of my daughter, stepson, stepdaughters, and grandchildren. Our grandchildren who live in California, haven't seen the cabin yet.

Table of Contents

Girly Creek

Donna G. Hendricks

The Cabin

at Girly Creek

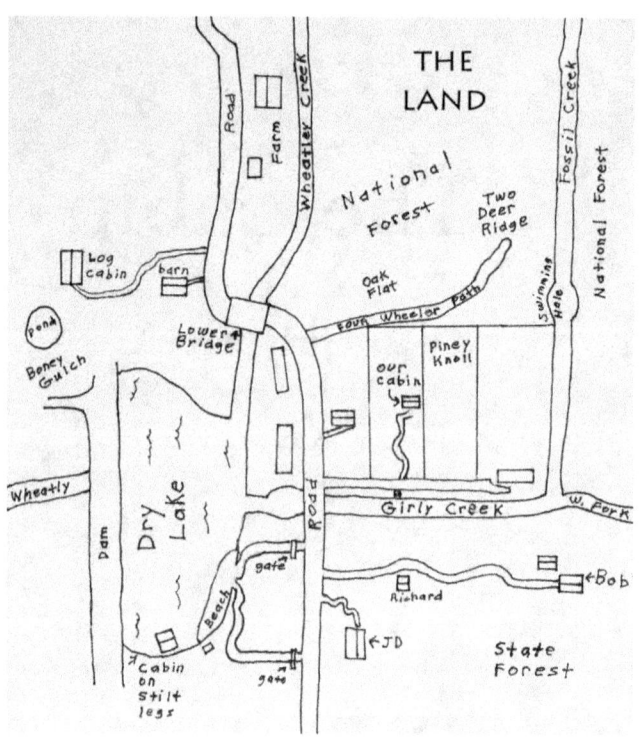

Map of The Land

1 WHY A CABIN?

When I was growing up, I spent my first 19 years living in the small town of Elberfeld, IN. A few trees grew in our yard, and I loved it when a rabbit appeared. My parents weren't nearly as happy about the rabbit because we had a garden. I longed to see more wildlife, such as deer, foxes, and all kinds of birds.

I guess I had wanted to build a cabin for a long time. My first experience with building was when I wanted to build a little house or cabin when I was a kid. I had found a book at our small town library that gave simple instructions on how to build one. A lot of old wood was piled in our garage basement, and Daddy always let me use a hammer, hand saw, and nails; therefore, I proceeded to build it. He happened to walk out to the backyard when I was struggling to get the frame to stand up.

He decided to build me a playhouse, using whatever he had. Daddy called it "making do." He used the wood from an old outhouse, extra shelves from the fruit cellar, and the leftover wood in the garage basement. Using panes of reclaimed glass, he made small windows that opened and closed. The leftover tile from our kitchen, now appeared on the floor of my playhouse. The small green shutters he made imitated the shutters he had created for our house which he had built too.

So I ended up having my own getaway place. I loved it and my friends came over to visit me there, and we often pretended it was a cabin or a museum. I wished it had some trees around it. Every time I planted a little tree, Mother would cut it down. She liked everything neat and probably didn't want more leaves to rake. I knew that a woods was free and natural and unplanned, and I would have one someday.

I collected miniature cabins for a long time and read books about cabins. I loved Helen Hoover's book, *A Place in the Woods,* about their journey to living in a cabin. Also I liked Louise Dickenson Rich's book, *We Took to the Woods* and Anne LaBastille's book, *Woodswoman,* about building her own cabin.

When I was grown, I wanted a getaway place in a woods. At one time I built a small cabin in our back yard next to our neighbor's woods. I had collected windows, a door, wood, and library books with instructions how to build a cabin that time too. The cabin is still in our back yard, sadly neglected; although John added on a porch and a steel roof to preserve it.

John was born in Phoenix, Arizona, and they lived right in the city. His dad wanted to move to Montana, which was really kind of hard since they had four children. They left their house, and with their camper moved to Montana, staying in a hilly, wooded area by Canyon Ferry Lake until they found a small log cabin to rent in Unionville. After a few months they rented a house, eventually buying a house with 1 ½ acres next to the Helena National Forest in Unionville.

When he was growing up, he loved to play in the woods and climb the huge mountain in the national forest. John took me to Montana a couple of years ago on our Western trip, and we hiked up part of this mountain. John and his youngest sister hiked on up to the top of a ridge of rocks! The rocks looked like children's huge building blocks thrown randomly on a pile. I couldn't believe they had the nerve to climb up there. Wow!

In Montana when John came home from school, he would grab his gun, if it was hunting season, and head for the woods. He hunted with his dad. They shot deer and elk, providing their family with meat, and he said moose were around too. The only reason for them to kill an animal was for food. John learned a lot about the outdoors from his dad. We looked into the underground root cellar that his dad built to store vegetables; and we were happy that it still survived after 50 years, and that the present owner wanted to keep it. John remembers digging a carrot garden with his mother, finding an old beat up ax head when he was digging. This ax head graces our bookcase.

Among John's favorite books are *Living the Good Life,* written by Helen and Scott Nearing and *The Wilderness Cabin* by Calvin Rutstrum. This book tells how to build a cabin. Also he likes *A Sand County Almanac* by Aldo Leopold, who said, "There are some who can live without wild things, and some who cannot." We both love Bradford Angier's books.

John loves the outdoors and has wanted a cabin out the woods for a long time too.

2 LOOKING FOR LAND

When we had decided we wanted to build a cabin, it wasn't easy to find the right property. The land we wanted would have a body of water such as a creek, a lake, or a river. The best thing would be if it was located next to a national forest or state land, and we hoped there would be some pine trees. Most of the property we found was too expensive, too far away, or didn't meet our general requirements.

John, Ben, who was around 10 or 11 at the time, and I drove to Jasper to pick up the realtor; then driving to Paoli, IN, we looked at some property--five acres along Hwy. 150. It had a driveway, a natural spring, some pine trees, and the Hoosier National Forest was behind it and on one side of it. There were rock boulders in the front. Although we liked it, the price was twice the amount we had saved, and it was way too far away.

Next, the three of us drove to Tell City to look at five acres that were for sale. We met Peggy at the Circle S Gas Station, following her to the property. The lane into the property was extremely steep, seeming to drop straight down into the hilly woods. Behind it was the Hoosier National Forest. The camp area included a shed, an outhouse, and a natural spring. There was a creek with a waterfall running through the property. Peggy took us for a walk in the woods, and we really were enjoying it until the gunshots hit the trees above us!

Peggy said it was probably the neighbor man shooting into the woods. What a scoundrel! He wanted to buy the property himself, but at <u>his</u> price! Before, when they had tried to sell it, he drove a fence post into the middle of the lane so no one could enter. He wasn't the kind of neighbor we wanted. Too bad. The property was beautiful, but we thought it would be hard to bring in supplies to build a cabin with that steep lane, and we couldn't tolerate a neighbor like him.

Another time my daughter, Shirley, who was about 15 years old at that time, had fixed us lunch before we left, but she wasn't interested in looking at the property with us. It seemed ready to rain as John and I drove there.

The realtor had given us a map of property for sale near Oriole, IN. There were twelve 10 acre wooded lots. We were interested in lot #1 because it was at the end of the road, and the Hoosier National Forest lay on three sides. Driving back to the lot on a newly rocked road, we discovered the rocks came to an end about 3/4 the way back. We stopped there and walked the rest of the way.

We loved lot #1. It was wooded and there were a couple of rocky streams running through it. There was an open meadow along part of it, and one side of the Hoosier National Forest was all pine trees. A ridge overlooking a stream with the pine trees in the background was the place where John said would be a perfect place to build our cabin. I agreed.

It was drizzling and becoming dark, so we walked back to the car. We cleaned the mud off our boots and got in, preparing to leave; however, when John put our Tracker in reverse, nothing happened, but the tires spun. There was deep mud in front of us, so we couldn't drive forward. We worked and worked, adding gravel under the tires, and doing everything we could think of for 2 ½ hours; but we couldn't back it up the hill. Even the four-wheel drive was not sufficient on the slick mud.

It was cold, dark, and raining, and we were far out in the woods. We weren't prepared to walk that far; but as we did both have plastic raincoats and gloves, we decided to walk into Oriole. We didn't have a flashlight with us, but we could see the road winding through the woods enough to be able to walk.

The town was small, and there weren't any businesses. Passing a house with a confederate flag flying, we read the sign in front saying, "Trespassers will be shot; survivors will be shot again." We kept walking.

We came to a house where we heard a lot of dogs yapping, and they were all running toward us!

"Good grief," I said. "We don't even have a stick in our hands to defend ourselves."

I totally expected to see a bunch of Doberman pinchers coming to attack us; but when they came into view, they were all friendly dogs, including some beagles, following us to the house. The lights were on, smoke was spewing from the chimney, a truck was sitting in the driveway, and we could see fans rotating inside; but no one came to the door. I wondered if I lived way out there if I would have.

Finally we came to the third house and an old man answered our knock. We told him about our problem.

"I couldn't help you. I just have an old car, but there is a man down the road who owns a big four-wheel drive truck who can," he said. We thanked him.

At the next house, a smiling man walked out to the road.

"Keep walking. He lives at the next house," he told us. We thanked him and continued walking.

When we came to that house, the man stepped out, inviting us inside for cookies and a hot drink with his wife and young son. The neighbor must have called everyone! Their Christmas tree was lit up, and we really enjoyed their company. He said he had a firewood cutting business.

Then he drove us back to our Tracker, pulling it up the hill with his big truck. We were so happy, and we finally talked him into taking $10 for his help. It was worth much more than that to us, but that was all the cash we had with us. What a nice man; I'll never forget him.

We found a pay phone and called Shirley to tell her why we were late. This was before anyone had heard of cell phones. She had been worried.

When we called the realtor back about buying the property, he said we could buy it as soon as they had logged it. We knew we wouldn't want it after the trees were hacked down.

Shirley and I had owned a camper, renting a lot at Yellow Banks Recreation Center in Selvin, IN, where it had been parked for the last three years. There was a lot of wooded property around a big lake--a nice, safe place for us to be outdoors.

John hadn't seen it yet, so we took him there. Since we wanted to build a cabin and planned to go to lots of other places, we decided to sell it. When we were there, mowing the grass and cleaning up the camper, John and I heard there was a cabin for sale. We weren't sure we were interested in a place on rented property, but we wanted to check it out.

Shirley was on spring break, and she had been wanting to visit Yellow Banks. John took the day off, taking Shirley, her best friend, and me there for the day. The girls were going to walk around, and so were we.

John and I wanted to look at the cabin we heard was for sale. It was a nice-looking cabin, but someone had already bought it.

Next we looked at some property near Hwy. 37 that included a big old barn, a lake, and several acres; but there wasn't a house or cabin on the property--only a house trailer. We loved the barn, and the property was large with a lot of woods, but I didn't want a trailer. It was way too expensive for us to build a cabin and buy all this property too, so we marked it off our list.

Later we met a realtor, Denny, on Hwy. 37, following him to the property way out in the country on a curvy road. First there was a scattering of houses, then only an occasional farm. We passed a woods with a lot of pine trees. After driving by the property that we recently checked out with the barn and trailer, the road dropped down a steep, steep hill, turning right where the paved road became gravel, and curving around fields and woods. Finally the realtor slowed his car in front of a yard, turning into a dirt lane.

Our first impression of the property was not that good--we had to cross someone's yard on a dirt lane to get to it, and there were a few old abandoned house trailers standing around on other properties.

The property we had come to see had four acres in all. In the front was one acre, which he said had been a farm field, where small miscellaneous trees and wild flowers now prospered. There was a little pond surrounded by redbud trees, and a lovely musical creek full of pretty colored rocks was flowing along the west side of the property with wildflowers blooming along its banks.

"I love this!" I said.

Behind this, the property rose quickly up a steep hill, then flattening out somewhat. These three acres were wooded and hilly with a few pine trees and lots of cedar and oak trees, which eventually adjoined the Hoosier National Forest.

"This would be a great place to hunt," John commented.

John liked that the property was hilly and adjoined the national forest. I liked all the redbud trees that were blooming and the yellow and purple wildflowers along the creek. Later I discovered the purple flowers were wild phlox.

The best part was that there was a large lake,

Dry Lake, across the road to which we would have access. The original owner had been a farmer, owning a lot of property and the lake. I believe he raised cows, and the ponds were dug for them to have fresh water to drink. When the farmer was old, he decided to sell the property, breaking it up into four acre lots. He wanted to give the people who bought these properties use of the lake.

After Denny unlocked the gate, we walked on a curvy, rocky lane with him to the beautiful lake, with lily pads, large white birds, bass, bluegill, catfish, and a huge grove of green cypress and pine trees growing on its other side.

We could just imagine building our cabin in the woods, sitting by the creek, and canoeing on this lovely lake. The price of the property was about what we had saved, so we followed Denny to town to sign the papers.

He gave us our own key to Dry Lake's gate, and he said an old rowboat came with the place. We're going to build a cabin!

Arrowhead Found at Girly Creek

3 THE LAND

A Gift from the Creator

A thin sliver of waxing moon struggles feebly against encroaching darkness.

Various birds say good night to all neighbors around about

Frogs sing their night songs.

Coyote voices in the darkness are raised in chorus, reaching many crescendos.

Two or three unseen geese, joining in, enthusiastically announce their arrival,

Rushing down the valley to the lake where their friends return loud greetings.

The flickering, crackling fire warms us as the chill, gusting south wind seeks to wrap us in its tentacles.

Light and sound blend with after dinner sedation, warming our bodies and our souls.

Returning the next weekend with Ben, we admired our land. Ben loved it too. Right away we saw our little creek that gurgles and tinkles like little bells--a soothing sound, running along beside the lane while we were driving to our property. One thing we noticed was that occasionally we would hear a donkey, a cow, a horse, or a rooster. I loved these country sounds instead of the sound of people yelling or heavy traffic!

There was a house next to our property, but there were many trees in between. An ancient trailer crouched across the road from us, but it didn't look like anyone lived there. A kid and his dog played in the yard of an old trailer down the road. A couple owned the empty lot right next to us, and another couple owned the property next to them with the big ugly house trailer, but they weren't there.

We hiked all over that land. Walking along the creek we found fossils laying around in it, and one day we found the source of the fossils. There was another creek flowing through the Hoosier National Forest, and there were a lot of fossils in that area. They seemed to come out of the side of the hill that the creek eroded into. Mostly we found crinoid stem fossils and fossilized shells; sometimes, we would find a large flat rock full of small fossils. A creek from higher ground that John called West Fork also ran down. Where these two creeks came together, they created a waterfall, pouring water into our creek.

Tramping over the hills, we saw two deer looking back at us as we walked by, so we named that place Two Deer Ridge. We called another place, The Glade, because there weren't any trees there--just wild flowers and small plants. The place where we found the large flat square rock, we named Table Top Rock. Rocky Gorge was a rocky place carved out by erosion. A level place, where a lot of oak trees grew, was Oak Flat. We called a path worn by four-wheelers, Four-Wheeler Path. Later on we named a wide deep private place we found in the creek, Swimming Hole. We called the creek with fossils in it, Fossil Creek, and the place with lots of pine trees, Piney Knoll. The whole thing, our property and all around us, including the lake and some of the national forest, we called The Land.

We hiked back to the Hoosier National Forest, finding a farm where they were logging. There was a tree marked "STOP" (with spray paint) at the edge, and John hugged it because he was so glad they had stopped. We saw a lot of different kinds of trees: dogwood, persimmon, buckeye, hickory, oak, pine, and walnut to name a few.

A gorgeous sunset glowed across Dry Lake that day, creating a pretty pink reflection across the water. We spotted two black cormorants, long-necked birds, sitting in a dead tree, and a great blue heron flew away! Walking across the dam John held my hand. The soft hills surrounded us. What a beautiful place! I couldn't believe it was ours to use! It's like a paradise to me. We ate the picnic lunch we packed, staying until dark, then headed back to the city.

The next time on the way to The Land, we stopped to buy a topographical map of the area, a local phone book, and a road map. Thus armed we headed for our place. We saw a white deer stepping into the woods on the way.

Heading for the lake, a large shiny blue pool lay on our right next to the road, inviting us. The creek ran under the road, digging this pool as it dropped from the culvert. Using our key, we opened the gate to the lake, driving up the lane to it. Graceful horses of different colors grazed on our left. The boat that came with our property was chained to a tree; it looked like it needed some work!

We put our canoe into the lake, exploring all around, and passing some lily pads and bushes. The lake had swollen to 20 acres. It was called Dry Lake because in the summer it would shrink to 10 acres, and then in the rainy season it would grow huge! John took my picture sitting on a beaver's house in the lake.

"Look at me and smile," he said. I did my best. It was fun sitting in such a strange place.

We paddled up Wheatley Creek in our canoe, and the water was so clean we could see the fish swimming in it. It finally became shallow, so we stepped out to walk up it. It became deeper, and as I had on long pants, I told John to go ahead. I would look for special rocks.

He immediately returned.

"I want to show you something, get on my back," he said.

He carried me piggy back, so I wouldn't get my pants legs wet, showing me some wildflowers--star-shaped red flowers were growing by some gnarled tree roots. So pretty. Later we looked them up, and they were called fire pink. We walked under a bridge which as time went by we named Lower Bridge, and John felt like this was a special place.

"And they lived happily ever after," he said. He skipped rocks across the water.

We walked back through our property, eating lunch by the neighbor's waterfall. While we were sitting there, we noticed that the bottom of the creek under the waterfall was solid rock.

"It would make a good place to swim," John commented. "It wouldn't be muddy." I agreed.

There was a deer path from up the hill, meandering through the grass down to the lane on our property, crossing the creek and climbing up the other side, off into someone else's property. I cleared it a little more down the embankment to the creek, picking up sticks and pulling weeds. John gathered some big flat rocks, building steps on our side of the creek, so we could walk down this path and step down gracefully to our creek without getting muddy. We hoped the deer would continue to walk this way too. There were already some ferns growing next to the place he built the steps. It looked so pretty.

"Our first improvement on our property!" I said. It was getting late, so reluctantly we left for home.

On the way we stopped at a gas station named Michael's, eating potato logs and chicken livers.

Michael's also sold deer licenses. Then we headed for home.

John, Ben, and I walked along Wheatley Creek, cutting through a farm down to Upper Bridge. Returning we walked on the road. The farmer was making bales of hay with a machine, a hay baler I think, and the whole family was helping. I found a piece of an Indian relic, laying in a field.

I love to think of the day we canoed all over Dry Lake. There was a small cabin, sitting up on stilt legs by the edge of the lake, but we didn't see any clues that anyone had been there recently. It would have been fun to see the inside, but the legs didn't look stable. Besides it wasn't ours, and it was probably locked.

Canoeing to the other side of the lake, we explored, circling around the cypress trees. The needles were frilly and soft-looking that time of the year. We also could see a small camper off the lake apiece; it appeared to be damaged, but we saved that for another day. Bushes and small trees stuck up in the water, and tall wildflowers with white blossoms grew around the edge of the lake. Some butterflies were interested in something in the rocks of the lane, but we didn't know what was attracting them.

Back to our property, John and I hiked all over. It was hard climbing up the steep hill behind the pond--I had to hold onto little trees to elevate myself. On the way up the hill, we saw a "sick" coyote, so we kept our distance. A hidden pond, back in the woods, was full of lily pads and bluegill. The area around the pond was carpeted with some short evergreen plants. I tripped on a green tangled sticker bush, greenbrier, I think, scratching my leg. Leave it to me to be clumsy.

When we arrived at our creek, we heard a crash, and a deer ran away. We saw another deer up the hill behind our property. We took a dip in the creek--what a relief--the water was so refreshing.

Jessica, my stepdaughter who was about 15 at the time, Ben, and I gathered rocks from the creek for the fire pit. Walking around in the creek was a lot of fun, but a lot of work too. We were having trouble pushing the wheelbarrow full of rocks up the hill.

"Dad, we can't get up the hill," Ben said. So we pushed and John pulled, moving it up the hill.

It was a pretty sunny day. We all worked on arranging the rocks around the fire pit, making a bench with flat rocks.

After building a big fire in the pit, we cut small

branches off a sassafras tree, peeling off the bark. Green sticks don't burn in a fire. Then we roasted hot dogs and marshmallows stuck on the sticks, having a picnic to celebrate our success. A cute little chipmunk was running around, disappearing into a hole in the tree next to us. Coyotes howled!! It was the first time we had heard them, and we seemed to move closer together. It was an eerie sound . . . Also there were frogs croaking and Canada Geese flying to the lake.

One day, we packed up and went camping at The Land. I had fried a chicken and made macaroni salad at home, so we wouldn't have to cook after we were there. I brought sheets, a blanket, and pillows because we didn't have sleeping bags yet. We set up our tent, lounge chairs, and food on the mowed part by the dry creek bed. Our creek had dried up for the summer, and it was nice and cool. A deer walked in the meadow behind the trees, crossing the road and walking toward the lake, so we followed.

When it was dark, we built a campfire, roasting marshmallows, and making s'mores. Then we crawled into our comfortable bed in the tent for the night. It was cozy.

We met JD, who lived next door. He asked us if

we would like to see the inside of his house. We did. The front room had a high ceiling, and there was a loft bedroom above the kitchen. The kitchen was an open square of cabinets, refrigerator, and stove. The table and chairs were arranged by a window. The living room, kitchen, and dining area were all in one large room, and there were open stairs leading up to the bedroom. A beautiful Indian rug hung on the wall, and an Indian basket with a horse painted on it graced an end table. JD's fly rod, rods and reels, and bow were hanging around in the big room.

JD was a writer for outdoor magazines. His dog, Girly, a German shepherd with one blue and one brown eye, came inside too. She was a friendly dog, so we decided to name our creek after her. It became Girly Creek at that moment!

Later we walked down to Lower Bridge, then down Wheatley Creek toward the lake. There was still water in this creek, and at one point we were hot, taking a dip.

Ben showed me how to fish for bass with a rod, reel, and a lure; and I had some success with this. I loved being able to jerk the lure along just so, attracting bass-- they thought the lure was something to eat! John had showed me how to fly fish, which was a lot more complicated, but I loved the flies he made himself. Up until that time, I only knew how to fish with a bobber and a worm. Our friend's husband at Yellow Banks had shown Shirley and me how to set the bobber and advised that we use a size 8 hook for bluegill. With my new knowledge, I could really pull in bluegill and bass!

Ben caught a large mouth bass in the lake that weighed almost 5 lbs. JD took Ben's photo holding the big fish, sending it to a magazine where his friend, Nina, was the Editor. We met her one day when she was visiting JD. Ben's picture holding the fish was published in the magazine!

John and I decided to hike over behind the dam on the far side of Dry Lake to see what was there. Wheatley Creek shot out of the overflow of the dam, moving fast! John said that would be a good place to fly fish. Walking along, we came upon some old concrete steps and an Osage orange plant. John said it was probably the remains of an old house. We found a deer skeleton, naming this place Boney Gulch. Hiking up the hill, we discovered a pond. John thought that it was an old home site.

Another day, we returned to the boisterous

Wheatley Creek behind the dam, fly fishing. John had made us Wooly Bugger flies, using black feathers, chenille yarn, and wire. I didn't catch anything. He caught a large fish, but it managed to escape with the fly.

John parted with his tiny brown Toyota, buying a full size Dodge Van! He decided to do this one time when we and our kids all wanted to go to Holiday World together. We all wouldn't fit into either my Tracker or his Toyota, so we had to drive both cars--not much fun when you can't ride with your sweetie.

So if we three wanted to spend the night at The Land, we packed up our huge van. Ben slept on the back seat of the van, and John and I slept in the back. Sometimes it was really cold out there, especially after having sat close to a roaring fire for a couple of hours. A few times we added a tarp onto the back, setting up a folding table; so we had a place to sit and eat.

It was on a spring day, almost like the one when we first saw the property, that we brought John's mother, who lived in Missouri, to see it. The redbud trees were blooming beautifully.

My stepdaughters, Sarah and Becky, drove up to see The Land. There wasn't a lot to see yet, so we rode over to Dry Lake to show them the view. It was always spectacular!

Shirley and her best friend also came by to see our property. Her friend's uncle owned a Christmas tree farm nearby, and the girls were old enough to drive over from there. They wouldn't budge off the lane, so they didn't see the creek or the lake. I have to admit, it probably didn't look that exciting to them--so far there were just a lot of wildflowers and trees.

We looked in the woods on the other side of our lower pond, seeing some lovely bluebells decorating it! Another time we saw a lot of yellow lily-type flowers with spots all over them. I looked them up and they were trout lilies. Also we saw bloodroot, with pretty white pedals, a yellow center, and frilly leaves. Why did it have this terrible name? I found out it contains a bright red juice that can be used as a tonic or stimulant.

Ben, John, and I built an outdoor cabinet for pans and other equipment that we might need to cook on the fire. We had found a big wooden box in our garage at home. It already had a back on it and a couple of shelves inside; so we set it on flat rocks, handy by the fire pit. Cutting doors to fit, we attached them with hinges, inventing a method to keep it closed. We used some sheets of aluminum we had to cover the roof. Later I painted the cabinet with camouflage colors, so it would blend in with its surroundings.

Bringing a grate for the fire pit from home, we cooked on it and kept the coffee pot warm. John split some wood, stacking it on a woodpile. Later we collected more flat rocks to lay on the bare dirt around the fire pit and cabinet. It looked like a little outdoor room.

The kids couldn't go with us this time, so John and I went to The Land alone. After breakfast at Hardy's, we drove on, and right before we were there, we stopped at a garage sale, buying a paper towel holder for the cabin of our dreams.

It turned out that their house--a three story A-frame, decorated with barn beams and creek rock--was for sale. They showed us the inside, and we really liked it, but it had a lot of stairs to walk. A couple of sheep were standing in a pen behind the house. They gave John a couple of boxes of Backpacker Magazines, which made him happy.

At The Land, John nailed a bluebird house he made onto a tree because we had been seeing bluebirds around. I hoped that they would move into it. I planted the red tulips that he had given me for Valentine's Day around the base of the tree.

The white-throated sparrow was singing! I could listen to it whistle its tune all day long--I loved it! Sometimes we had heard a young sparrow trying to learn the song, and it was so cute to hear.

Some lovely violet colored wildflowers were blooming along the lane. According to a wildflower book, they are called cancer weeds, *salvia lyrata*, not a very pretty name, but the leaves were said to be used externally for cancer.

I had decided that every time we came, I was going to dig up two buckets of small rocks from the creek and pour them on our lane, so it wouldn't be so muddy. I dug up my two buckets full that day.

We built a campfire and ate stew for supper. We invited JD over for dessert--cherry pie and coffee.

I drove to Vallonia, IN, where the Southern Indiana State Nursery was located, to buy 100 little pine trees for The Land while John was at work. It had been raining at home, but it was nice on the rest of my drive. I came home with 100 trees. A few days later John, Ben, and I planted the little pine trees all through our woods.

Later we returned, and while Ben was fishing,

John and I checked on and watered the trees. We also looked at the wild flowers, pond, creek, and fire pit.

We loved all the trees, but we wished for more. Driving to Vallonia, we bought some pawpaw trees and northern bayberries, trading six of our plants for six cypress trees with another customer. We had a lot of exercise planting all that stuff.

On Thanksgiving we went to The Land to hunt and camp, taking a meal cooked at home and a homemade pumpkin pie.

I accompanied the guys hunting a couple of times, but I wasn't armed. Ben had completed his Hunters Education class, so he had a gun. We all dressed in camouflage, rubbing some stuff on our faces, so we would blend in with our surroundings.

Ben and I sat in the woods, and John circled us, trying to scare something toward us. I loved sitting out in the woods, seeing all the trees around us and the sky above, anticipating whatever! A squirrel bounced through the trees, having a grand time--he had no idea we were sitting there! We tried not to blink or turn our heads. There were crows flying over our heads, and once we saw a deer in the distance. I spotted a strange tiny insect--maybe I was the first person who'd ever seen it!

Yeah, right. Ben thought he saw a bobcat! It was really cool "being invisible" for a little while.

On the way home John stopped at a gas station to buy us some soft drinks. Ben and I were sitting in the van, when someone walked by staring at me. I realized that I still had the dark stuff smeared on my face. She probably was thinking I was a bank robber!

When I went coyote hunting with the guys, we all wore camouflage clothes and sat still. Ben blew the distressed rabbit call. It was exciting sitting in the woods, seeing and hearing everything around me and not knowing what would show up. We finally heard coyotes howling in the distance. Also we heard frogs and Canada Geese. No coyote ever came our way, so the guys were disappointed. I would have liked to have seen a coyote out in the wild, but I didn't want to see it killed.

Ben went hunting for a goose. John and I sat by the fire pit while he hunted. We had heard a couple of shots and were waiting for him to show it to us.

He came walking up.

"Dad, I shot a goose, but it fell on Dry Lake. The lake is frozen with a thin layer of ice!" he said.

John borrowed JD's rowboat, and they went over the ice--Ben inside and John pushing the boat. I stood by the edge of the lake, wringing my hands; I was so worried John would fall through the ice! What would I do if it happened? There wouldn't be time for me to get JD to help! We didn't have cell phones yet then. I was even looking around for a long branch that I could hold out for him to grab onto if he did fall through.

They found the goose. I was so happy when I saw them rowing safely on the deeper side of the lake where it wasn't frozen.

The next night we roasted the goose at home, and the three of us ate it for supper. It was the first time Ben and I had eaten goose. It was delicious!

Ben invited me to accompany him when he hunted for squirrels. We were walking along in the woods, when he spotted a squirrel. He handed me his gun! I was surprised--I thought <u>he</u> was going to hunt. He motioned (go ahead).

I held the gun, aiming it at the squirrel. I shot it, and it ran off. I was so upset--wounding it seemed so much worse to me than killing it! Now it was hurt, I didn't know where it was, so I couldn't help it if it was suffering! The guys felt bad also. If I had killed it, it would have been food, which is what should happen after hunting. I will probably never shoot anything again.

4 LIKE A COUPLE OF HAPPY DOGS

Like a couple of happy dogs,
we roam the hills and woods
seeking the hidden paths,
to explore and look for deer
before returning to
our camp with its
comforts of a crackling fire,
singing teakettle,
and warm foods.
Surrounded by the trees,
there are many wonders
for us to see and hear.

It took a while to decide what kind of cabin we wanted, and how big we should make it. At first we thought it should be more like a shelter with three sides and about 13'x13' square.

We decided to look for a spot for our shelter.

First we walked to the lake, to the trailer that's for sale, and down the road. A neighbor was hauling some rocks out of Wheatley Creek with a four-wheeler and a trailer. We saw a female turkey with two chicks. John spotted a deer in the distance.

"We are like a couple of happy dogs looking around," John said.

Scouting around in a plowed field, we looked for arrowheads but with no luck. What fun! You know, we never picked a place for the shelter that day.

Friday after work we packed up the van and went to The Land for the night. John attached a tarp at the end with some poles because it might rain. We set the folding table under it. It was a little warm and buggy.

After breakfast we walked up the Four-Wheeler Path that turned into an old logging road behind our property. John and I looked for the boundaries of The Land.

While we were looking, we also kept an eye out for goldenseal. One time when we were near Fredericksburg, IN, we ran across a fellow drying yellow root out in the sun. He said he sells it. We looked it up, and it was another name for goldenseal. It bears a single red berry in the summertime and is used as an antiseptic, a laxative, or to stop bleeding in herbal medicine. We read that it can be poisonous if taken internally in large doses.

Also we looked for ginseng, which is a perennial, slow-growing plant with three large leaves and two small leaves, usually growing on north or east slopes in moist hardwood forests. I think it's mainly the root that people are after. In many states looking for ginseng is restricted to a certain seasonal time period. In some places you can't look for it at all. It's an endangered species because of over collection. Companion plants include trillium and bloodroot, among many others, which we have at The Land. It bears a single red berry too, but I don't know at what time of the year. We didn't have any luck on that, but we did find hickory nuts and three turkey feathers. Box turtles seemed to be everywhere.

While John was looking for a place to set up a deer stand, we spotted a buck and a doe. Walking down the steep hill, we passed both our ponds, getting all scratched up. John was covered with tiny ticks!

When we thought about all the work it would take, we decided to make the cabin a little larger while we were at it. After a lot of thought, we decided to make it 16'x16' with four sides instead of three.

After choosing a flat spot on a hill next to the lower pond for our cabin, we cut down the small trees and brush in that area. We spent a lot of time making sure the area was square. After spreading plastic, John and Ben drove stakes to mark the corners.

Then we realized that we needed a Building Permit, so we drove to the court house. We were given the name and address of the person from which we could purchase the permit, but we were surprised when we pulled up in front of a house. The lady who answered the door told us to walk around back.

When we approached the back of the house, she invited us to sit on the back porch. She sat at her desk asking us questions, filling out the permit. The family's black pooch was playing in the yard, and the wash was hanging on the clothesline. It wasn't what we expected, but it was an interesting experience, and we had a Building Permit.

We cleared a driveway to the building site from the dirt lane, cutting down small trees, digging out roots, and smoothing it out. John said he would like the driveway to curve around the trees, instead of making it straight. I agreed that would be more attractive.

While we were doing this, a teen-age boy with rather long black hair and a tan, strolled up. He told us his name, saying he lived in the trailer down the road. We all talked for a little while, and John mentioned that we were clearing it for a driveway.

"Could you pay me to haul the rocks?" he asked.

"Do you have a driver's license?" John asked.

"Yes," he answered.

"Do you have something to haul it in?" John asked.

"No, I'll use your vehicle."

John looked at our van, shaking his head. He couldn't imagine letting a young kid we didn't even know drive our van to Tell City to buy rock, and we didn't own a trailer yet.

"We don't have a trailer. Sorry."

We ordered a small truckload of river rock to be hauled from Tell City for the driveway. They spread it as they dumped it.

A man from R.E.C. talked to us about getting electricity for the cabin. We either had to buy an electric pole, which he said was very expensive, or dig across the neighbor's yard, which we couldn't even imagine digging up. We never did get electricity.

I wasn't too disappointment that we couldn't get electricity. I really never wanted a TV, electric lights, or a radio in the cabin. In fact those are some of the reasons I wanted to get away! I loved hearing the melodies of the birds and all the country sounds, such as a rooster crowing. I loved to be able to see the bright stars at night—"the diamonds in the sky." They wouldn't be nearly so bright if there were a lot of electric lights around. I loved the peace and quiet at The Land.

Randy, the neighbor who owned the house trailer, came over one day. John showed him some of the plants we had bought at the nursery. A lot of our plants hadn't made it, but Randy was interested in buying some plants too.

John was temporarily laid off, so he had some time to work on the cabin, and he studied a pole barn book. He dug holes with a post hole digger 24 inches deep, laying 10-12" of concrete in the bottoms. Setting 6"x6" poles in the holes, he filled them with rocks and more concrete.

Each step in building the cabin, took us a lot of time. First we had to save the money to buy whatever that step required, then it took us a lot of time to do it. We didn't have electricity, so we used hand tools. It was summer time, it was hot, and we drank a lot of water to replace the sweat.

Building a wood frame for the floor was a hard hurtle to cross. We bought six 2x10s, hauling them to our property in the back of the van. John drilled holes, bolting them to the upright poles.

After we finished this part, we brought boards from home to make joists, using some used boards given to us by my brother-in-law and sister. We cut the joists to size, using a hand saw. I remember some of them were slightly too long, so I filed them down using a wood rasp. Finally the joists were made and ready to install.

While we were working, a big rabbit who we named Thumper, hopped down the hill and sat watching us for a while. Several times a turtle, who we named Myrtle, strolled down from the pond to watch us. She came so often she wore a path in the weeds. One time we saw her walking up her path, and she was all muddy. Later we saw her sitting in the pond, and another day she walked down our driveway.

Several times we saw deer in the distance, running across the meadow. Once we found a place where the foliage was smashed down, looking like a couple of deer had spent the night. Wild turkeys lived down by Wheatley Creek, and a mother deer and fawn walked down the road.

JD had his eye on a house down the road. The man who owned it had died, and JD showed us the house, overlooking Dry Lake. We had to drive up a steep driveway to get there to see it. The house was large, and besides the usual rooms, there was a big room with windows suitable for an office--JD would have a place to do his writing. He said it also had a basement, and there was a roomy garage too. It had a lots of woods around it, and the Indiana State Forest was behind it.

We nailed down the OSB for the sub floor of our cabin. We were proud of our accomplishments so far, especially since it was done in very hot weather with no electricity, running water, or air conditioning.

A couple of times we camped in a two-man tent, so we wouldn't have to drive home when we were working on the cabin. We set the tent up on our cabin sub floor. On the first night, John was awakened by coyotes yipping in the meadow, but I slept through it. The second night both of us were waked up by deer blowing (their emergency call) nearby. Scary sounding . . . It felt to me that they didn't like us on "their" property and were trying to scare us away.

Sometimes we would hear a barred owl. We've always heard that their call sounds like "Who cooks for you?" It's true.

One day we stopped at a garage sale and were able to buy a lot of windows, including a casement window that the people had bought for their daughter's house; but she didn't use them. We bought them for an extremely reasonable price, and we were really happy.

Bird Nest in the Outhouse

5 HIRING HELP

On our way to The Land, we usually drove up I64 to the Hwy. 37 turnoff; but that day we decided to turn sooner, taking a look at a nearby town, Bristow. We saw a small grocery store on the left. Stopping at a church that was having a yard sale, we looked around to see if there was anything we could use in building our cabin. We didn't see anything like that.

"Does anyone know a carpenter who could frame our cabin?" John asked a lady.

"My husband is a carpenter," she answered. "He's the Pastor; he's over there." So we followed her to meet the Pastor. He did construction work on the side and was very interested in our cabin, especially since it was close to Bristow.

The two men talked it over, and the Pastor said he could come to our place on Saturday to make an estimate. John gave him instructions how to get there.

So he came Saturday, along with his teenage son. We told him that we wanted a 16'x16' cabin with a sleeping loft. The floor was already built, so he just needed to build the building on it. We wanted him to build the frame, cover the outside with OSB, and roof it. He said he and his son could work on it every Saturday.

We told him about the windows we had bought; he said he would use them, and we explained what we had in mind. I can't stand a place without windows, since I worked at a job for five years that didn't have any. The whole inside of the building where we worked was gray, and I worked in a cubicle by myself! It drove me crazy!

Since we didn't have any electricity, he said he would bring a generator, saying he would call with an estimate.

He called and we were happy with what he was charging us. Our biggest problem with building a cabin was that we didn't have a lot of extra money after the bills were paid, but it was our desire to have one. He said he would order what was needed, and it was delivered to our driveway. They came the next Saturday to begin.

We couldn't seem to stay away from their

working on the cabin at The Land, so we showed up from time to time. By November, the Pastor had framed the first and second floor including the roof frame. The first floor had OSB on the sides.

John trimmed the cedar tree where it was rubbing up against the cabin. I threw the cedar branches on "the thicket." Thumper (the rabbit) came running out.

A huge flock of Sandhill cranes flew over, circling above us for a long time. We could hear their voices, like they were discussing over and over where to land and were trying to make a decision. Eventually they landed at Dry Lake.

The Pastor had measured the windows we had bought at the garage sale and planned places for them. We were delighted when we could see where they were going to be located--we would have a wonderful view! Another day we visited, bringing a plastic outdoor table and a couple of chairs; so we could sit and admire the view and what was done so far.

Eventually they added a sleeping loft that we could climb up to, using a ladder. In January, the Pastor finished his part of the cabin.

It was hard to climb up to our front door on a board. My balance wasn't that good, so John found some wooden steps and used conveyor belts from his workplace. We could walk into our cabin like civilized people, and the muddy paths would be covered with the conveyor belts.

We temporarily installed the wood stove with the pipe sticking out a window, wrapped the bottom half of the cabin with Tyvac, and installed some windows. The Pastor came to help John wrap the top of the cabin and install the upstairs windows.

Ben wasn't coming with us much anymore. He had grown into a fine young man, had a job, and had his own buddies. He visited occasionally to see how we were coming along.

After we bought insulation and staples at a hardware store in Jasper, IN, we insulated the inside first floor walls. It took a lot of time to staple the insulation onto the 2 by 4 studs. Then we both worked on nailing up the pine paneling, using some free wood that had been used in shipping crates to John's work place. They told him at work that he could take as much as he needed if one of the other workers didn't get it first. It took us quite a while, sawing it, and nailing it on by hand. We still liked the idea of not using electricity when we worked. We didn't have electricity in the cabin, but we could have bought a generator. John thought the pine paneling looked a little uneven and knotty, but in my opinion it looked great in a rustic cabin.

When we were finished with that, we worked on nailing down a wood floor on top of the OSB. We didn't do it all in one day, that's for sure. He would work on it until he tired of it, then would go do something else. Then I would work on it for a while. Finally, we had it all nailed down, and John coated it with polyurethane, using a paint roller. We moved everything to one side and did half of the room at a time, giving it two coats. We thought it was beautiful!

John installed the woodstove in its permanent place, cutting a hole in the ceiling and the roof for the chimney pipe. The stove sat on a metal floor guard, made for this purpose.

The cabin was lit with kerosene lamps and candles. A two burner propane stove took care of our basic cooking needs, and we kept the coffee pot warm in the winter by setting it on the wood stove.

We brought large jugs of water with us when we came to the cabin. After buying a plastic sink, which was really meant to be used for washing laundry, at a garage sale, we set a bucket under the drain pipe to catch the runoff water.

When I planned to wash dishes, we heated the water on the propane stove or on the wood stove in the winter. A white board covered most of the opening on top of the sink. I washed the dishes in a white enamel pan trimmed in red, rinsing them in a similar pan, and draining them in the dish drainer, which was arranged so the water would drain into the sink. Afterwards I would take the bucket outside to throw out the dirty water. I believe we were living as our ancestors probably did when we were staying at the cabin. I can't say that I would like to live this way all the time, but it was fun for short periods.

The furniture was mostly bought at garage sales, thrift shops, or given to us by a friend or family. We picked out a large round pine table with three matching chairs in a rustic style, painted with orange shellac. Later we found some other high-backed vintage chairs at a garage sale for $1.00 each.

I built a pine cabinet using some of the leftover free wood. My dad was a carpenter, so I spent a lot of time in the garage with him, watching him drive a nail, and using a hand saw and a jig saw. He didn't talk much, but his actions spoke volumes. Soon, I was building stuff too. I loved the knotty pine look, so I varnished the cabinet with orange shellac. I took my Amish table that was the same color as the cabinet to the cabin, setting them next to each other as a kitchen work space.

We stopped at a hardware store in Dale, IN, buying some white enameled brackets. Nailing them on each side of the small casement window over the pine cabinet and Amish table, we cut boards to make three shelves on each side to hold dishes, dry food, canisters, and jars of food. Not too long after that, we bought some clear plastic boxes to protect our dishes and utensils from the critters. We hung the larger pots and pans from the rafters.

Deciding to use my parent's old Adirondack double chair for the couch, I made a pad for the seat, adding cushions on the back to make it comfortable, and draping my mother's hand crocheted afghan in colors of green, gold, and white over one arm. The coffee table was a short shabby chic drum table I loved, bought from a thrift shop. A side table was an old handmade table with turned legs that John treasured, having been built by a friend, and it had been his kitchen table before we were married. I laid a small gold and white checkered cloth over the top because I thought it went with the afghan, setting a kerosene lamp and a few knickknacks on it. Also we brought a bookshelf from home, and I made a small bookshelf from leftover pine. We brought a lot of books and magazines, filling the book shelves, so there would be reading materials at the cabin. We screwed some antique hooks onto the wall next to the door, for hanging coats and hats, and brought an old wooden medicine cabinet with a mirror.

Our next door neighbor at home had passed away, and her nephew bought her place. He asked us if we were interested in her old desk with a chair. I remembered the desk well--it was in her living room for as long as I could remember. She liked to paint, so she had painted it black; then she painted it gray. It might have been other colors too, before that. I was interested in it, so he gave it to us, and it came to be a part of our cabin.

At Christmas, when we drew names, our relatives would buy us something for our cabin. They gave us a pretty large round rug, a kerosene lamp that hangs on the wall, and a teapot with four mugs with a different flower painted on each one that we will always treasure. We were given an oval green and rust-colored braided rug that I laid in front of the couch and a basket made from woven cloth.

We had found curtains at a garage sale for five cents a panel. It was near the end of their sale, and they had reduced the prices, so they wouldn't have to haul everything off, the lady told us. They were white shear curtains. There were so many windows in the cabin downstairs--I'm not complaining, mind you, I'm thrilled--eleven counting the window in the door. We still needed more curtains, so we bought some at thrift stores. They were all very similar but not an exact match. At first we temporarily hung them on wire with the ends wrapped around a couple of nails. My friend had given us some brass hooks. We placed them about ½ way down from the top on either side of the large windows, so we could pull the curtains back in the daytime. It looked great!

For a time I collected moose objects. It all began when we took John's mother for a drive down the Kancamagus Highway when she was staying in New Hampshire, and I wanted to see a moose. We kept seeing signs saying, "Moose Crossing," but we never saw a moose. After we were back home, she sent me a postcard with a picture of a moose on it. Then I received a lot of moose items from the family for Christmas. I believe someone must have put a bug in their ears about my liking moose! Most of these items were at home, but a window hanging with branches of pine, a ribbon and a moose is still on our cabin door, and a mirror with moose and pine trees decorating it continues to grace our cabin.

We weren't finished with the upstairs. The floor was still OSB, insulation was installed on only part of it, and the paneling wasn't all up yet. We managed to get my parent's old bed up there--climbing a ladder and moving furniture at the same time wasn't always an easy thing!

I made the bed, covering it with a handmade quilt. Later we added a top layer of plastic, tucking it in all around to keep out the critters. We hung an old rustic quilt on the wall behind the head of the bed. It was made of simple plain-colored square blocks of wool material sewn together, and it had a stitch of gold thread tied in the middle of each block. We had bought it at a garage sale for $1.00! I loved it.

A battery operated lantern with a handle was hung over our bed, so we could read at night. We used a rustic dresser with a drawer that I had built a long time ago, hand painting designs on the front of the drawer. I set an old gold framed mirror on top. Rag rugs, bought at a garage sale, lay on the floor. We found a couple of heart-shaped end tables, and a couple of long poles that we attached to the attic ceiling on which to hang our clothes. Vintage off-white drapes were hung at the windows on each end of the room. I built some utility shelves with some of the free wood. We set a bucket with a lid upstairs in the bedroom to use as a chamber pot when we needed it in the night.

The hills behind the lake across the road had turned red from the sunset before dark! Everything around us seemed to echo--a car driving down the almost empty road, coyotes howling in the distance, turkeys gobbling, barred owls calling . . . It was all I ever dreamed of.

We spent our first night at our cabin. A whippoorwill that seemed to be right outside our window, said its name, "whip-poor-will, whip-poor-will," half the night. I believe it was meant to be a welcome call.

JD sold his house to Tom and his wife and their cute little girl, and he moved down the road to the house overlooking Dry Lake.

John and I were fishing in Dry Lake and not

having much luck! The water was pretty high and Wheatley Creek was high too, so we canoed up it apiece, fishing along the way. We both caught our limit of bass that day and enjoyed a feast back at the cabin! I don't think fish ever tastes so good as when we catch it ourselves!

Becky and her fiancé, Louie, took a plane from California to visit family. They came out to see our cabin. I think they really liked it even though it was still pretty rustic, and we had a long way to go. The four of us hiked along Girly Creek and then up Fossil Creek. We showed them where we found the fossils. Louie loved the creek.

After they had visited everyone, we drove them to the airport in Louisville, KY. After we saw them off, on our drive back we stopped at the Goodwill in Corydon (we couldn't seem to pass up the shops).

We looked out the cabin window at the pond next to it, wishing it would hold more water. Rain water would run down the hill into the pond, but there had to be a leak somewhere because the water ended up on the lower land below the pond. The cypress trees were probably watered this way.

So buying some bentonite, John decided to

repair it. We dug the pond out the best we could, using shovels when it was dry, and John filled holes with the bentonite.

The next time we spent the night at the cabin, it rained steadily, and I noticed the pond was filling up. I told John, and we stood outside when the rain had slacked, admiring our beautiful pond full of water! We were so happy! Maybe we could stock the pond with a few bluegill.

When we were lying in bed that night, after John was asleep, I heard something outside, hopping across the roof. I wondered if it was a squirrel. What could climb up there? Could it be a rat? Oooooo. My imagination always wandered when I couldn't sleep.

The next morning when we looked out the window, the pond was almost dry.

The 17 year cicadas came out and were crawling all over our trees. We found trillium--three petals and three leaves on each wildflower--back in the woods. I just loved them, so I dug up a couple of them (leaving the others so they'll continue to grow there), planting them in front of the cabin. I returned to the place where we found the wild irises, digging up a few of them to plant around the stone steps by the creek.

We, and our other neighbors, who we seldom had seen, were having trouble driving to our properties after it rained because of the muddy lane. Sometimes we had to park up on the road when it looked too soft to drive through. The neighbors who lived around us told us about the creek rising and covering the road at least once. Several times when we came, we saw evidence of high water because there were piles of leaves and driftwood in a line way back on our property.

Getting together with Randy and Danny, we rented a front end loader from the nearby town, Jasper, to dig gravel out of the creek to cover the lane. John decided to first lay black plastic on the lane that went through Tom's property and on our property to keep weeds from growing there. The other guys didn't want to spend that much money on their properties, so they didn't buy plastic. The men elected John to drive the machine, and they spread the rock over the lane, smoothing it down with shovels and rakes. John did a good job, digging that rock with the machine! They did have some trouble with it breaking down, and it had to be worked on, but they finally finished. We haven't had trouble getting to our properties since. No more mud!

There were always critters trying to get into the

cabin. One time it was full of lady bugs!! We think they were the Asian variety, and they were hiding behind everything in the cabin! In the spring, John sealed up all the cracks, and we don't have that problem as much anymore.

John walked up to his hunting spot, and I beachcombed in the lane. I was walking along, looking at the rocks when I saw a point sticking up. It looked like it was made of flint, so I reached down to pick it up --it was a nice arrowhead with only the point nicked slightly! I gave it a closer look--it was made of Indiana Hornstone, the same kind of flint we found at Stagecoach Campground by the Blue River.

When I thought about it, John had dug the rock on the lane from the creek! I wonder how many years ago, an Indian had walked down Girly Creek, quietly, so he wouldn't scare off the game. He had shot at something, hitting it with the arrowhead because it was nicked. I wondered what it was, a deer? He hadn't found the arrowhead afterward because it was still with the rocks.

I worked inside. I had finally collected enough

curtain rods to replace the wires holding up the curtains. Today I planned to change all that.

After I took down the curtains, the wire, and nails, I realized that each frame needed a strip of wood between them, so I could hang the rods level. First I made a search around inside the cabin, then under the cabin, finding enough scrap wood to do it.

One of the curtains was ripped! I sewed it up. Every job at the cabin always turned out bigger. Oh yes, nails. Where would we keep the headless nails? Searching around, I found some left over from the paneling job, so I sawed the wood, nailing the pieces in place. Now for nailing up the brackets. A few went up easy; then I came to one that just wouldn't work! Oh, I dropped the nail behind the settee, so I pulled it out.

Oh, poor little lizard! Some kind of a green lizard was dead--caught in a mouse trap! I picked up the nail. I'll bury the lizard later. The next time I tried to hit the nail I hit my left forefinger. Ouch!! Not to be stopped, I continued and flattened the bracket instead. Rats! Do we have pliers? I looked around without success.

It's time for a break. I hadn't even looked at Girly Creek since we'd been here today. I spotted two tiny pine trees growing in the driveway. Girly Creek was full of water, moving along, with the sun sparkling on the water. I loved the sound. Thus refreshed I went back to my job.

John showed up and asked me to walk to the lake with him. I pointed out the pine trees I found and the creek on the way. He loved the way Girly Creek looked, and we got some exercise walking to the lake and back.

I decided to hang a few baskets we had around the house on the cabin ceiling. I had visited a lady who had her kitchen ceiling covered with all kinds of baskets, and I liked it. As friends and family came to visit our cabin, they began giving us their extra baskets, and some gave us new baskets for gifts. Now our ceiling looked as good as hers did.

Then, I kept finding so many pretty rocks and fossils in the creek, in the driveway, and by the lake; I kept a basket for them, displaying them and a large mussel shell on the windowsills. Found feathers were kept standing in a jar.

We did finally meet Randy's wife. They came for a couple days at the same time we were staying at the cabin. We really liked her, and we could tell they were really comfortable together.

It was about this time that I decided we needed an outhouse. John's hands were full at this time, and he didn't think it was as important as I did. I decided to build one, and I wanted to build it at home in our garage, so I could use the power saw. There was a lot of wood sitting around in the garage, so I found wood for the sides and door and for the seat. I cut all the pieces at home, taking it all to the cabin where John helped me to put it together and set it up.

We put it above the pond on a hill, down from our fire pit. Attaching the door with a couple of hinges, we added a latch to keep it closed. I used some of our aluminum to cover the roof. I brought a medium-sized tub to set under the hole, filling it with dry leaves and sawdust--kind of like a composting toilet. I decided I needed to buy lime to sprinkle over it.

It wasn't very fancy, but it was definitely more private than out in the woods! I made an opening in the back, installing a flap on hinges, so we could remove the tub when needed.

My mother-in-law came to visit us at home for a couple of weeks, so we brought her for another visit at the cabin. While she was there, we built a fire in the wood stove, sitting around in front of it on our chairs. She loved it!

"This reminds me of Montana," she exclaimed. John's family had lived there for several years when he was growing up.

She wasn't interested in looking around outside. --she liked sitting and talking about old times so much-- until she needed to use the restroom.

"We have an outhouse," I told her.

Luckily I had recently swept it, and there was toilet paper in it. (Later on, I discovered that I had to keep the toilet paper put up inside the cabin, to keep squirrels from using it for nesting material). I walked her back there, and stood outside the door for our return.

When she stepped out, she was telling me something, waving her hands while she talked--I can't recall what--but she almost toppled off into the pond. I grabbed her as fast as I could--for a second I thought we were both going over--she was heavier than me! But I got my footing, managing to hold on to her. In my head I could see us rolling down the hill together, splashing into the pond! Good grief! I'm glad THAT didn't happen!

We took a few deep breaths, then we shakily walked along the path, making our way down the hill to the cabin.

After she left to go to Indianapolis to visit with her daughter, I had a plan. One day John and Ben were working on their hunting stands, and I was puttering in the cabin. I thought about his mother and me climbing down the hill from the fire pit to the cabin. It would be nice to have steps. We had gathered a pile of big flat rocks from the creek on another day, so I got the idea to lay steps up the hill.

I was working on my idea when JD and Girly walked up.

"I'm taking Girly for a walk. Would you want to walk over to the lake with us?" he asked.

"No, I'm going to do some work around here," I answered. "But thanks for asking."

JD said goodbye and I petted Girly, and they walked away. I began building the steps. The rocks were very heavy, and it was hard to set them so they were steady on a hill. John and Ben were walking toward me.

"What are you doing?" John asked.

He took over building the steps, and you know, we have beautiful, steady, rock steps up to the fire pit that also leads to the outhouse trail!

I made a flower bed on the south side of the cabin by setting creek rocks in a rectangle. Inside it, I planted a wild fern and a wildflower I found, and I brought starts of iris, daylily, rose of Sharon, and Easter flowers from home. It made a nice flower garden. A few dogwood trees were growing among the swamp oaks and redbud trees around the cabin.

John was hunting, and I was puttering around fixing up the cabin. I was nailing on a board when I noticed a doe stroll by, looking up through the window. I was surprised that a deer would come so close while I was making so much noise, and I wished I had taken a picture of it. I decided to clean the cabin windows so I could if the occasion arose. Later I was making a lot of noise when I noticed several deer out in the meadow next to us, congregating like they were holding a town meeting. Were they discussing what I was doing? When I was hanging a picture, a buck with a big rack ran by the window on the other side of the cabin.

After a long day, John finally walked in the door. "I haven't seen a deer all day," he complained.

"It's no wonder," I said. "They've all been hanging

around the cabin all day!"

Finally, a contractor friend of ours had some used siding left over from a job he was completing; it looked sort of camouflaged with subtle shadings of off white, gray, and dull light green. John had worked for him for a while, so he paid John back with the siding. I liked it much better than if it had been bright white! It will fit in with our woods.

The Pastor brought his scaffolding, so he and John could side the cabin. His son had found a job and was no longer helping. It was a lot of work because there were many windows and a door to work around, so there were a lot of cuts to make. When it was finished, we were so happy that the cabin was finally covered with siding after years.

6 PLACES TO GO

Often when we stayed at our cabin, we took day trips to surrounding towns, rivers, and other places. We wanted to see what was out there!

"That cloud looks like a wizard with ears, tail, and two long legs," I said.

"That's steam, not a cloud," John said. It was coming from an exhaust stack.

We had decided to take the scenic route to the cabin that day, eventually driving by the two big chimneys with the "wizard" steam pouring out of them near Rockport, IN. Then we saw the red caboose that houses a Mexican Restaurant. Having eaten there one time, we thought it was really cool dining in the caboose.

John saw a building with large glass windows in front.

"That would be a good place for a photo studio," he said.

"Why are you interested in it having such big windows?" I asked.

"It's all about light."

We drove through Grandview. We had seen a huge riverboat docked there a few years ago. Also a nice park is right by the river where we have eaten a picnic lunch a few times, beachcombing along the river.

At Troy, a small town by the Ohio River, we looked around an old house which overlooks the river that was for sale. There was a front door, but no porch or anything was under the door to step onto, so it appeared that the person would fall to the sidewalk below!

I walked down to the river to beachcomb and look around while John was photographing an old house. When I strolled back up I saw a couple of motorcycles parked at the top. Bikers, I thought nervously!! Here I was by myself! But as I came closer I realized they were a clean cut couple, and they were talking to John! I joined the conversation, and they told us about a couple of other fun places around the area to visit.

Another time when we were at Troy, the river was flooding, and the street called Water Street was covered with water. We visited a very old style hardware store and looked around a retreat way up on a hill overlooking the river. So many explorations!

At Tell City, We visited the US Forest Service, and John bought a topo map of the Little Blue River. We shopped at a junk shop, buying an old handmade egg basket and a coal shovel, both for the cabin. I asked about the miniature log cabin.

"I worked on this little cabin for over 40 hours, and I'm 87 years old," the owner said. "You couldn't pay me enough money to buy it."

"It's wonderful," I said. "I don't blame you for not selling it."

"I whittled these animals too."

"I love them. Could I take a photo of you with the log cabin and animals?"

"Sure. I'd like that." So I took his picture. He and John had a discussion for a while about some tools. He was a nice man.

Afterward, we drove to the small hunting shop to buy our fishing licenses.

We took Highway 66 through Cannelton, shopping at a yard sale where we bought a quilt stitched with deer print material and plain brown and green material in between the patterned blocks. I thought it was perfect for the cabin.

John shot a photo of an old cotton mill which had been remodeled into an apartment building. The Cannelton Cotton Mill, built in 1851 and declared a Historic landmark in 1991, produced cotton sheeting and batting. Mostly women and girls had worked there.

After a while we were hungry, so we drove across the Ohio Bridge to Hawesville, KY to the Riverview Restaurant. It was way up on a bluff above the Ohio River. Sitting right by the window, it seemed to me like we were hanging right over the river, seeing it far off in both directions! I remember there was a bird feeder in front of the window. We ordered quail and salads because we wanted to try something different. It was delicious!

Stopping at Rocky Point, we walked down to a little sandy beach by the Ohio River, watching a barge chug by. A campground full of camp trailers were parked by the river. We sipped hot chocolate at a little store that had a wonderful front porch that was sort of like a yard sale, with furniture, clothes, rag rugs, plants, aprons, etc. for sale. Above the porch was an open air dining room with picnic tables where a lot of bikers were eating lunch--their motorcycles were parked all over.

We came to Oriole, a town we hadn't seen in years where we had looked for help when our car was stuck in the mud, about 13 years before. We drove past what we thought was the house of the man who had helped us, stopping to look at it again.

"It looks different somehow," I said to John. "Is this the house?"

"Well, I thought it was here. Maybe it has been remodeled, or maybe it was torn down and replaced!" Driving around a little more, we decided that this house had to be it.

We wanted to see the 10 acres that we almost bought, but seeing the development after all these years was a disappointment. Right at the entrance a beat up trailer that seemed abandoned, was crouching in a grown up, weedy lot. A house was on one lot and a cabin on the next; but the lots were mowed, like in a housing development, with no personality, flowers, or trees!

Then we came to a sign saying, "Absolutely no trespassers past this point." There was a heavy yellow cord stretched across the road. We never saw the formerly beautiful 10 acre woods from all those years ago! We were so happy we hadn't bought into this property!

Returning to the road, which was curvy and sometimes had 90 degree turns, we drove on, finally arriving at the gate to Stagecoach Campground. We had to drive through a scary (to me it was scary, not John) stretch where there was a sheer drop down to a seemingly bottomless pit. It was all wooded and quite beautiful as we neared the beach that I always loved.

At the campground, we walked down the lane to the Blue River. The river water was lower than usual because of the lack of rain that summer, and that made the beach even bigger! I remembered other times when the beach was almost covered by water.

John shot photos and looked at his photography textbook while I combed the beach, eventually finding part of a gorget! It's a stone ornament an Indian probably wore for decoration, hanging around his/her neck on some sort of string. The ornament usually had one or two holes drilled in it and was made of shale or slate. The piece I found was made of slate and didn't have a hole in it

Also I found a curved piece of flint that was chipped along the edges. It was about three inches long, and it looked like it was broken off on one end. We ran into a fellow later who thought it was a paleo knife. I have found photos of artifacts on the internet that were curved like mine, but one was called a scraper. Paleo tools are old, so are these? I wish I knew more on the subject.

I was carrying my bag of finds when I met a woman digging in the gravel. She said she was looking for Indian beads. I knew what she meant--I've looked for them myself many times. Holding one up, she showed me a fossilized crinoid stem. She was as enthusiastic about them as I was about artifacts. Her name was Terri. She said she's looked for them there before. It was nice talking to her.

Another time when we were there a few months later, a couple, wading in the shallow water around the beach, each carried a net and were trying to catch whatever. There was a new boat ramp. I found another piece of the gorget that fit together with the piece I had found before, except it had a hole in it! It looked like I needed one more piece to complete it! Also I found a core, a cone-shaped piece of Indiana Hornstone, that I believe someone had chipped off pieces of flint to make arrowheads or tools.

One time at Stagecoach Campground I was looking for fossils while John fished. I did find a lot of unusual fossils. One looked like it could have been part of a pipe, but I didn't believe it was. It seemed to be something natural, not man made.

After eating our picnic lunch we brought with us, we watched a couple of people, paddling their canoe toward us, and landing on the beach. We talked to them, and I recall that his name was Ronald, but I don't remember hers. They said they ran a little shop in English, IN named Sun Oaks. We'll have to check it out sometime.

Then we had eaten an early supper at the Overlook Restaurant--it overlooked the Ohio River. The food was delicious! We watched two barges pass each other on the curve of the river out the window as we ate.

Once we drove down a steep lane to The Dock, a cool restaurant in Old Leavenworth. There were some old buildings sitting around the area left from the flood of '37. I noticed a couple of motorcycles pulled up as we were parking. Since it was so warm, they were serving outside on the deck. It was the first day they were open that year, so things were moving slowly. There wasn't much in the food line to choose from, but we were happy to be at this place, munching grilled whitefish on white bread, kettle chips, and slaw. A motorboat puttered up to the beach, and the couple walked up to sit at a table. Then some people rode by on horses! There was certainly a lot going on here. It became our favorite place to eat when we were in that area.

Another time when we were eating there, a big thunderstorm was occurring, so we had to sit inside to eat. I didn't think it was nearly as much fun just looking through the glass!

After we ate, we hiked along the Ohio River, beachcombing. It was an interesting walk, and we saw a barge moving down the river. Then I found a mussel shell with a round hole cut out of it and was wondering why the hole was cut.

Then we stopped at a store in Leavenworth where they had an old button-cutting machine that cut buttons out of a shell just like the one I found! The shell had a round hole cut out of it too. The owner of the store said there had been three button cutting factories there around 1920. A lot of interesting things were for sale in the shop, and they served food too. We decided to have dessert while we were there.

John and I drove to the rifle range at Sugar Ridge. I remembered our visit there to shoot before we were married, and I hadn't shot much before that. I aimed carefully.

Afterwards he said, "Hi, Annie Oakley." I smiled. I guess I did okay.

Today he needed to try out his newly bought "used" shotgun. It was fun; we were next to a group of hunters who talked to us. It was a noisy place! We wore ear plugs, but it didn't help much. Then we moved to the shotgun range where John wanted me to practice loading the gun and shooting at a box (self-protection training).

We took John's cousin and his wife to see the cabin. On the way we stopped at Huffman Mill Covered Bridge outside of Bristow, IN. The bridge, built in 1864, was spanning the Anderson River.

They liked the cabin. We all walked along Girly Creek and at the falls, turned and walked up Fossil Creek through the national forest. He found a big fossil that we think was originally part of a fossilized tree limb or root. Afterwards the guys hiked up the hill behind the cabin while we visited inside. Later they said he used the fossil for a door stop at their house.

After church our friends, a couple we met in our Sunday school class, John, and I went to Bristow for the Fall Festival. On the way, we drove through the town, and besides two churches, there was a small post office. I mailed a letter there at one time--I hope it's still open. There once was a restaurant, but it wasn't there the next time we looked. A long time ago we stopped at a thrift store in a small building, buying a couple of things, and the guy gave us some walnuts from a tree across the road. Later at home, we set some of the walnuts on the front porch for our squirrels. They carried them off, and I noticed the squirrels digging holes in our yard to bury them. I wondered how they would find them all back, but I guess they didn't--we have several walnut trees now.

We ate lunch at the festival. I remember we were sitting by a picnic table, eating sausage sandwiches. Walking around, we looked at the car show, which my friend's husband especially liked. We saw the Pastor and his wife at the flea market where there were lots of things for sale.

There was also a demonstration showing how sorghum molasses used to be made. I think there was a mill in the middle where they fed in the sorghum cane. A horse was attached to a pole, circling around it. I bought us each a sorghum molasses sucker. Then we took our friends to see our cabin and the lake.

We drove to Huntingburg, walking down 4th Street, window shopping--lots of antique shops! The only store open; however, was the Hispanic grocery, so we entered, buying a Hispanic coke, black beans, vanilla oatmeal, a scrubber, and a 5 cent ring.

Then we ate at Grandy's Restaurant. On the way to the cabin, we drove through Jasper, shopping at the St. Vincent DePaul, Salvation Army, and the Goodwill thrift shops.

When we finally arrived at the cabin, we decided to drive to the restaurant in Leopold for pie and decaf coffee, and then to the cabin to sleep.

The next morning we drove to a Flea Market at Corydon. There was a lot of things to pick from, but we didn't see anything we had to have. Then to Tipsaw Lake for a dip while Ben fished. We ended up walking around the Lake on the Discovery Trail. A storm blew in, the thunder boomed, and darkness was approaching. It was a longer trail then we thought! Upon finishing the trail, we were all starved, so we raided the cooler.

Returning to The Land to pick up the canoe we left another day, JD invited us over. He told us about how Girly hadn't been acting like she felt good, so he took her to the vet.

"The vet found a bullet in Girly's liver, but I never saw that she was bleeding. Someone must have shot her, but who? When?"

"So what are you supposed to do?" John asked.

"The vet never came to a definite conclusion. I don't know what to do! He said to wait and see if she starts getting better."

"I sure hope so; it seems like he could do something," John offered.

"If she's not better soon, I'll find a new vet!"

We finally left, arriving home at 11:30 p.m. What a day!

At the Little Blue River, we both fished. I caught a large-mouth bass with my fishing rod and a lure and hooked a second one, but it got away. John tried out his new flies he had tied; he caught a pumpkin seed fish with his fly.

John brought his map of the Little Blue River, and we found a place by it with a block house and garage that were all junked up. There was a path from it leading down to the Little Blue. The trouble was, it was right next to I64 and the noise was bad! We were walking around, talking, when suddenly a man, unkempt, tattooed, and possibly drunk, burst out of the bushes, heading toward us. He about scared me to death! But he talked to John a few minutes before wandering off into the trees.

We drove to Grantsburg, entering the Hoosier National Forest, and hiking along a trail through a pine forest and up a hill. It dropped straight off and down below us snaked the Little Blue. It was beautiful! It reminded me of a scene in the movie, *Deliverance,* when a guy was standing on a cliff overlooking the river. Several deer ran off. Walking through the pines we spotted a couple of deer skeletons. Right when we were returning to the car, it began raining, so we decided to head back.

Another time when we were looking for the Little Blue River, we pulled into a lane. There was a house on the left, and closer to the river sat an old house trailer. John wanted to look at the river, but he thought we should ask first. We knocked on the door of the trailer, and. a little lady answered the door. She was very friendly, stepping out on the porch with her little dog. We introduced ourselves, and she said she was Mrs. Enlow.

She didn't mind at all that we wanted to look at the river; in fact, she walked down with us, sitting in her swing near the river. She told us she had lived there for years and about the horses she rode as a young girl. When she married, they moved away but later had returned to this place.

"If we brought our canoe, could we put it in here, so we can paddle down the river?" John asked.

"Sure," she said. "Lots of people canoe down here." We talked some more, then we needed to go. The view of the river was beautiful from her place. John later said he wished we owned it.

We stopped by to visit Mrs. Enlow over the years, and she always remembered us; but one time when we came, she wasn't there. We knocked on the door of the house next door. A lady answered the door, and we told her that we were looking for Mrs. Enlow.

"She's my mother," she said. "She hasn't been well and is staying with us."

She brought her mom in, but she didn't remember us. After Mrs. Enlow returned to her chair, her daughter said not to be upset that she didn't know us--she didn't recognize anyone! After we talked to her a little more, we left. We were really sad that our friend didn't know us anymore.

We happened by there the next year, and seeing a For Sale sign, we drove into the lane. Mrs. Enlow's trailer was gone. Her daughter wasn't home, but we looked around Mrs. Enlow's property one last time. There was some sort of an interesting out building that we hadn't noticed before. The price they were asking for the property was stated on the sign. We couldn't possibly afford it, but it just wasn't the same without our friend.

The closest town nearby was English, IN where we bought sandwiches at a gas station, eating them by a creek. I believe this was one of the creeks that fed into the Little Blue River. The town had to move up to higher ground several years ago because of the river flooding the lowland.

Eventually, we visited Sun Oaks in English, the shop that the couple told us they owned. Ronald remembered us. It was an interesting place, selling hand thrown pottery, handmade jewelry, molasses, wooden items, kites, old furniture, and all kinds of plants in the spring and the summer. They built their own greenhouse using a lot of old windows. We were really impressed!

A thrilling thing for us was the time we saw and heard a couple of otters swimming in the Little Blue. They seemed to be talking together and laughing. One had a high pitched tinkly voice; the other had a deeper voice. I would have loved to know what they were saying, but they were speaking Otter. They were playing in the water, having a wonderful time! Someone said they liked to slide down hills too. I had only heard bad things about otters before--how they depleted the fish population in the creeks and rivers--but now I know another side of them also.

We canoed many times in the Little Blue, but one time sticks in my mind. We were looking for a different place to canoe, and we could see our favorite little river off a bridge way out in the country. I couldn't even tell you exactly where we were.

Having taken the river canoe that I won in a contest (that's another story) off the truck, we slid it down the hill. It was a rugged, jagged steep hill, but we managed to get the canoe down and into the river. The water was beautiful, blue, and clear as we paddled along. I looked around at the totally wild, free place. No one came here--there was no trash littering its banks.

Near the edge of the water, some crawdads were walking around, holding their pinchers in front of them for protection, I guess or to catch food. A pileated wood pecker flew to a tree, pecking loudly. There was tall green grass growing along the edge of the water; big trees of many varieties decorated the woods around us.

A huge tree had fallen across the river, so we had to puff and grunt, finally dragging the canoe over it. We paddled down the river. John set up a scene to take a photo, and my job was to push the button on his camera when the time was right.

We had a wonderful day, but finally we had to turn around, struggling back over the fallen tree to head back. Then we were standing at the bottom of the jagged hill, gazing up. It looked especially steep from this angle, so we pushed, we pulled, but we couldn't get further than a couple of feet! We were stuck!!

Standing there, puffing and panting from exertion, we thought, what can we do? John came up with a plan. He backed the truck up to the top of the hill, tying a rope onto the bumper. Oh, I'm glad the truck had a real metal bumper and not plastic. He climbed back down, tying the other end to the canoe. Back in the truck, he slowly moved forward. The canoe would get stuck on places at times, so I would turn it just a little to get past it, as John moved the truck slowly forward. The canoe was finally dragged to the top of the hill, so John tied it on top of the truck again. Another adventure finished.

A place we liked to explore was the road cut where I64 and Hwy. 137 crossed. It was our fossil-hunting place. There is a high cliff on each of the four corners of the intersection. They are terraced, so we climbed from terrace to terrace to make our way to the top. I think I've only been all the way to the top one time, but John has climbed up several times.

We have found a lot of fossils and rocks at this place. Besides finding crinoid stems, we also have found the whole crinoid "flower." A crinoid is not a plant; however, it's an animal that had turned to stone after a long period of time from back when that area was covered with water. We also have found fossilized shells and plants. Once when we were there, we met another fossil hunter who showed us a fossil that was imbedded in a wall of stone.

John's youngest sister and her son came to see

our new cabin. After we had eaten lunch and had shown them around the creek and lake, we took them to the road cut. John, I, and his sister, were rock hounds in common. I remember when we were at their farm, she showed us the creek in which she loved to swim, and we all found rocks we liked. When they bought their house in town, she created a beautiful garden with rocks she found all around it. She also loves shells.

John read in the paper that there was going to be a Sohn Auction in Paoli, IN. They were selling the property of an artist and schoolteacher. So while we were staying at the cabin, we drove to Paoli for the auction. John won some tackle boxes and rifle cases.

I was thrilled to see a 1671 book, named *The Lord's Day*, on one of the tables among many other books. I had never seen a book this old before, so I was hoping we would still be there when it was auctioned--I was wondering how much it would bring! I was thinking about taking a photo of the title page, but I had laid the book down on the table where I had found it while I was looking at another book. A man walked by, grabbing the antique book, and walking quickly on down the aisle with it! I only saw him from the back--he was tall, had a pot belly, and was wearing a striped shirt. That describes a fourth of the male population, does it not? To give him the benefit of the doubt, he could have laid the book down on another table after I saw him, but his manner and the fast speed he was moving away made me suspicious that he was stealing it. Or another possibility was that they had hired him to watch expensive items, and he was just doing his duty.

I told John, and he informed the auctioneer who said to point him out to a person with a badge. I thought that might be him hanging around talking to some other guys, but I wasn't sure it was him. This guy didn't have a badge, so he wasn't a worker. When I glanced at him, he looked quickly away. Later when I swept my eyes around the grounds, I couldn't see him anymore. I guess this mystery will never be solved, but I do wonder about him.

I saw a large clay statue of a head that I really liked, but I didn't need. They had lots of art supplies: easels, canvases, oil paints, books, but I already had all of that. I enjoyed looking at the primitive and shabby chic furniture, but our house and cabin were full!

There were several Amish people bidding. The men wore slacks, medium blue shirts, vests, and natural colored straw hats. The women wore dark long dresses and black bonnets.

Walking through the large house, we could see that they could have had big parties. We definitely couldn't buy this house, nor was it our type of house; but there were things we liked about it, such as the fire places and stone chimneys. Walking through the garage, we could see a very old-looking basement.

We met our friends from our Sunday school class at Tell City for lunch. There were several places where we liked to eat in Tell City. So far we had eaten at Tell Street Café, Freezer, Ponderosa, the Knights of Columbus, and McDonalds, so it was a hard decision.

Then they followed us to check on the cabin. Afterwards we rode with them to Leopold to the visit the Country Store where we each found something to buy. I bought some hand cream in a dispenser bottle that smelled really good. We drove by the grade school my friend's husband had attended when he was a kid. Then we were off to Buzzard's Roost, a really high overlook in the Hoosier National Forest, hiking around looking at all the views.

We drove to Derby which was named after

Derby in the United Kingdom. The restaurant, where we had all eaten a buffet together before, was closed. All of us were really disappointed, but we noticed a pizza place across the street; so we bought a couple of pizzas, eating them by a picnic table next to the Ohio River. What a view we had!

After we parted, John took photos of some chickens we saw by a chicken house. There were also some big wild turkeys, hanging around.

Another day we camped at Sycamore Springs in English, IN, but there was a mistake and two sets of campers were signed up for the same campsite. They let us camp by Deer Lake, hooked up to the electricity. We were the only camper by the lake, trees and birds were all around, and it was very private. We fished in the lake; but catching only little fish, we threw them back. I loved the sound of the frogs croaking. We noticed they sang different tunes, like there were a variety of frog species, and it was like music to my ears.

The next morning we drove to Tell City for breakfast before going to the cabin. While we were there we visited JD, and Nina was there too. I really liked her, and we found we had a lot in common. I knew she was an editor for an outdoor magazine in the past. She said she loved to fish in the Little Blue River--she fishes there by herself. I don't think I would ever go there without someone with me! I told her about the time John and I were fishing at the Little Blue River, and we swam in the river. Then we walked down the middle of the river, fishing as we walked. Later, a woman showed us the furniture she built out of barn wood in a cabin near the river. She really did a good job, and she inspired me to want to build more furniture. Nina admired the blouse I was wearing, and we were discussing other things we had in common.

JD said he needed to finish a rush writing assignment for a magazine, so we didn't stay long. It was raining a lot, so we drove back to Sycamore Springs to pack.

One time when we were staying at the cabin, we drove to Louisville for a photo show and reception. Our former instructor at Ivy Tech Community College, Ms. R_____ had entered three photos, winning $500!

7 STUFF HAPPENS

This chapter tells about some of the funny, awful, unusual, and scary events that happened over the years. They aren't necessarily in order of occurrence.

Around this time we realized that we weren't seeing Tom or his wife next door anymore. Then we heard that their house had been repossessed. We walked over, and there was a realtor lock on their front door.

I had decided to dig up a fern to plant by the cabin, so I walked down to Fossil Creek with my shovel. A Baltimore oriole sat on a branch high up in a tree--it was the first one I had ever seen! I loved its orange and black colors. Also there were some wild irises. I'll dig some up to plant by our steps to Girly Creek sometime, I promised myself.

Finding a nice fern, I was digging around it

when I heard swishing noises, realizing something was charging toward me through the tall weeds, which were waving around in the air as it (whatever it was) moved toward me! I grabbed my shovel, running as fast as my legs would carry me. I could hear it panting right behind me! I finally knew I couldn't outrun it, so I turned around to face it, holding my shovel blade out in front of me like a weapon to defend myself.

Whatever it was, the animal was moving off through the tall weeds, which were shaking and waving around again. I didn't know what it was, but I was glad it had gone!

We were walking down Fossil Creek, when we caught a glimpse of something blue, lying on a leaf in the creek--it was a beautiful blue butterfly, but it was dead! We were stunned because we had never seen any butterflies around here like it! How did it come to be here? What had happened to it?

Looking it up in my butterfly and moth book, common American species, was useless--there wasn't anything like it in the book. So I looked on my computer. The closest butterfly I could find was a blue morpho, which was found in tropical rain forests of

South and Central America! Why would such a butterfly be in our creek?

Our granddaughter, Amelia, came with us for the day at the cabin. We walked over to Dry Lake, looking around at everything. There was some water standing, and she noticed that there were lots of little frogs jumping around; so she was running around trying to catch one. Finally, she did and was carrying a tiny frog in the palm of her hand. He wasn't even trying to escape. I called the tiny frog "he" because of her close attachment to the little guy.

After strolling over to Girly Creek, we sat on the stone steps, enjoying the tinkling of the creek. She loved the sound as much as I did, I think. The water was swishing past us, and the rocks at the bottom were really colorful. She petted the little frog carefully, trying to think of a name for him . . . or her. I can't recall the names she thought of, but they all seemed unusual to me, even for a frog!

Suddenly he jumped off her hand, diving into the water. We thought we could see him swimming down the creek. She was upset! I knew we wouldn't be able to catch him.

"He looks happy in our creek, Amelia. He can live here and will probably find lots of friends."

"But I miss him," she said.

Once when we first arrived at the cabin, it was almost dark, and we heard a sound upstairs! John shined his light up the opening.

"There's a flying squirrel up there!" John exclaimed. It disappeared in a flash.

The next day, when it was light and we could see better, John found a place upstairs where it had chewed a hole under the eave to enter, so he had another job to do. He nailed a board over it temporarily.

There was that time when we came to check on the cabin, and the door was standing open (even though we had locked it when we left). Something had broken some pottery bowls, pushed the globe off an oil lamp, and climbed upstairs, knocking over the dresser and peeing on our bed! Luckily, we kept the large sheet of plastic over the bed!

"What could climb up the ladder?" I asked.

"A raccoon or opossum," John answered. "We'll have to return with a latch and lock." I sat the dresser upright and picked up all the broken pieces, throwing them away. I set the globe in a safe place, and I cleaned the plastic on the bed with a rag and Lysol. Ugh! I mourned the two pottery bowls that were broken. They had been hand thrown on a wheel in the pottery shop at Yellow Banks, a place that meant a lot to Shirley and me.

John and I found an old "home site" in the woods. The reason we noticed it was there were Easter flowers growing around the area. They were probably planted by the people who once lived in a house on that property. The next time we brought our metal detector, finding part of an old stove, a hoe, and an iron. It was interesting and lots of fun--plus some work--to find a little bit of history that way.

We were digging rocks out of the creek to fill in holes of the lane. John had been filling the wheelbarrow, and pushing it to the lane. I wanted to do that too, so I filled the wheelbarrow about halfway with rock, pushing it toward the lane. There was a bump that I just couldn't make it over. I tried really hard and, woo-la, success! This was all well and good, except something didn't feel right in my lower back. That night I couldn't stand to lay in the bed because of a crazy-feeling pain in the shin of my leg. A few days passed, then I made an appointment with a chiropractor. There was only one chiropractor in town who was covered by my insurance, so I made my appointment with him.

I was diagnosed as having a sciatica problem. My chiropractor was very rough, in my opinion. It was my first visit to a chiropractor, so I didn't have anything with which to compare it. One time he caused my head to flop back without steadying it--then I had a problem with my neck too. I had noticed his other patients, when they walked into the waiting room, seemed to become worse instead of better as time passed. Finally, I wouldn't go back.

The ladies I worked with at the Girl Scout office suggested a lady chiropractor that adjusted them, so I made an appointment with her. I told her I had a new problem--I couldn't reach my feet or tie my shoes, so I wore shoes that didn't tie. She performed a different test on me, saying that I had a sacroiliac joint problem too, and I would be lucky if it was ever fixed. She did cure my sciatica nerve pain.

Seven years later I was walking with a friend, and she was telling me about her chiropractor. I told her about my sacroiliac joint.

"Oh, my chiropractor could fix that," she said. She was right. The first day he adjusted me, he made it all better! I could tie my shoes again, I could sit on the floor, I could pull weeds in my flower bed, and I could put on socks the regular way. Now, he's a CHIROPRACTOR! Praise the Lord!

We met Katy, the new neighbor who bought Tom's house next door. She was really nice and said she had MS; she had a grown son and two grandchildren. She said she's disappointed she can't see the lake from her front door because of the trees this time of the year.

I told her we had a cabin next door. She couldn't see it because it was surrounded by the woods.

"Does that lane lead to your cabin?" she asked.

"Yes. It goes down to our neighbor's house trailer too."

"Would it be alright if I drove my four-wheeler down to your cabin and the trailer? I haven't had the nerve to go out on the road yet."

"Sure. We don't mind. I don't believe Randy would care either," I said. I think that made her day. It didn't sound like she could get around much.

When we arrived at the cabin, we were greeted by a huge, aggressive tan dog that growled and barked at the same time. Its fur was bristling! We had never seen a dog act like that before, and it was on our property! It moved in on us, barking/growling!

John loves dogs. Usually when he met a new dog, he kneeled down to its level, holding out his hand, and it would sniff his hand before he petted it. I had never seen a dog before that didn't respond to him.

John had to throw a rock at it, so it would leave our property!

Later, we decided to take a break and walk to the lake. John had taken his handgun with us. On the way up the road, this dog appeared on a hill to our left. The dog was doing the same growl/bark thing as before. Then we saw the teen-age kid; he just stood there. Two smaller dogs had joined us and were nipping our heels.

"Call off your dogs!" John appealed to him! The kid stood silent just looking at us.

Then the big dog charged down the hill right at us, bristling, tail down, snarling. In my mind, I could feel its sharp teeth tearing my leg, already. Right at the last second, John shot it. It fell beside the road. In my opinion, because of the way the kid and the dog acted, that dog was trained to attack!

John called the sheriff, telling him he had shot a dog in self-defense.

"Are you going to investigate and file a report?" John asked him.

"Well, you said it was self-defense, so there's no need for me to come," he answered.

I think John wanted him to come and make a report. He told the kid he was sorry he had to shoot his dog. He certainly didn't want to kill a dog, but he just couldn't stand there and let it tear us apart!

Then we took our shovel up to the house where we thought he lived, knocking on the door. A lot of dogs inside were looking out the windows and door, barking. An older woman wrestled her way out the door, so as not to let the dogs out.

"We're moving in March," she said before we said anything.

"We just brought our shovel, so the boy can bury his dog," John explained.

She nodded, accepting the shovel.

We left. We never saw that kid, any of those dogs, or our shovel again.

I walked over to visit Katy. She was telling me that a neighbor's teenage son had been knocking on her door, asking if he could come in to watch TV with her.

"I don't think that boy is all there," she said. "I mean up here!" She pointed to her head. "And he wants to come in and sit with me?"

"Don't they have a TV?" I asked.

"Apparently not! Then I caught him looking in the window! I told him to go home!"

"So, you don't have that problem, anymore?" I asked.

"Oh, I still have it. Then he tried to break in!"

"Oh my goodness!"

"Yes! So I shot in the air to scare him away, but he wouldn't go. I finally called the sheriff!"

"Then what happened?"

"They came and arrested him, putting him in jail. Then he called me!"

"What for?" I asked.

"He wanted me to come to bail him out! Can you believe it?"

"He must not be all there."

John was setting up a deer stand near Fossil

Creek, and I decided to visit him to see how it was going. While I was a walking down the lane, I saw a young deer step out of the bushes across the meadow. I froze like a statue, so maybe it would walk on out. It did.

I stood still, and it walked on to the middle of the field, looking at me. Still I didn't move; finally, it walked over to the lane, standing in front of me, staring at me. It seemed to me it gawked at me for a long time! Having trouble standing still, I finally blinked! It jumped away, standing there looking at me. Then we heard a noise from the bushes. The little deer ran for all it was worth, jumping back into the shrubs. I wondered if the mother had called it and was there, waiting.

I felt elated, like I'd had a close friendship with a wild being. Smiling, I walked on down the lane to visit John.

We finally went to the cabin. When we arrived, the door was standing open again (we had locked it); but the piece of metal, that we had outside the door to keep the rain from seeping under it, was still there. We could see signs of mice, and the floor had bird poop splashed on it, like a bird had been flying around inside. While John went to check out his hunting spot, I swept and used Lysol to clean up the cabin.

There was always a problem about bathing at the cabin. Sometimes we would take a dip in the creek, take a spit bath, or clean up with fresh wipes. At other times we would drive to a gas station where we could pay to take a shower, and one time we showered at Celina Lake's shower house.

We had just arrived, and as John headed to the men's shower, I was walking into the women's shower room. A young nice-looking woman came in a few minutes later. There were two shower stalls, so we both took our showers. I was bathed and dressed before she was, so I stepped out the door.

Four rough-looking guys were standing around a big old ratty van--not readying themselves for showers--but seemed to be waiting. Four pairs of eyes bored holes into me as I walked by them. I tried not to look disturbed, but I was scared, walking casually to our truck. I unlocked the door, stepped in, nonchalantly relocking the door.

While I was waiting for John, the young woman stepped out. The guys were all watching her as she climbed into their van. Then they were standing around the van, preparing to get in when John strolled out. He spoke to them in his usual friendly way, while walking to our truck. I unlocked his door, and he entered.

Heading out toward the highway with the van close behind us, it seemed like their front bumper was glued to the back of our truck! Were they following us? It sure seemed like it.

"Are they following us?" I asked John.

"I sure hope not," he answered.

Finally, approaching the highway, we turned right to return to the cabin. I glanced back.

"They are turning the other way, toward the interstate," I said. I was relieved.

But what was that girl doing with those thugs? They didn't look like her kind of people, but she was obviously with them willingly. I guess we'll never know.

We heard that a 12-year old boy, while walking through the national forest on his way to visit his grandma, had disappeared. No one ever heard from him again. What could have happened to him?

One day, we drove down to visit JD, and the first thing we noticed next to his driveway was a brown, old-looking outhouse. WIMMEN was painted in light-colored letters on the front! That JD; he's always trying to be funny!

He had placed big flat stones, buried to the same height as the surrounding yard, leading up to the new porch. Several hummingbird feeders were hanging along the porch; and these birds were diving at each other, making buzzing noises, and trying to get their share of the food. JD had set a couple comfortable chairs and a stork sculpture made out of metal on the porch. The log rail running along the front of the porch looked really nice, and it made it look more like a cabin. We visited with him, watching the commotion the hummingbirds were making, and he told us that he had just planted the flowers in front yesterday. We agreed they were pretty.

I visited Katy. When we were talking, I noticed a wheelchair sitting over to the side of the room.

"I had to call the ambulance in the middle of the night--two different times," she said.

"Oh my goodness. Are you alright?"

"I am now, but I didn't think I was going to make it when I called them. I had an MS attack!"

"I'm so glad to hear they would come way out

here!"

"Me too, I didn't know if they would!" she said. It really worried me, her living out there by herself!

John and I spent a couple of nights at the cabin. He was sitting in his hunting stand, and later he told me he had watched a doe and a fawn step out of the woods. The fawn played in the creek for a long time, hopping around to see the wave action, and not noticing that John was there. A squirrel pulled itself up over a limb, looking eye to eye with him.

The second day he hunted in the afternoon. Snow began to fall, and I noticed his headlight laying on the table, realizing he had forgotten to take it along. Then I heard shots. He walked back, saying he shot a six-point buck.

We stopped by the cabin to check on it. The downstairs had the usual dead bugs and a dead mouse in a trap, occurring when we hadn't been there for a while; but upstairs was a total mess! We left the trail camera upstairs.

The first thing we both wanted to do when we arrived again at the cabin was check the camera we left upstairs. John had brought his laptop, so we could. The photo clearly showed two regular gray squirrels climbing around on our bedroom walls.

"We have to get them out of here, so we can finish the upstairs!" I said.

"They would be good for supper," John remarked, always the hunter.

Now that we knew we no longer had a flying squirrel, which is protected, we could shoot or trap them. We'd hate to do that though--we would love to have them climbing around in our woods, but not in our bedroom!

We decided to camp at Sycamore Springs in English, IN while we cleaned and repaired the cabin.

The next morning we ate breakfast at Swartz's Restaurant nearby. After driving to the cabin, John repaired the wood and vents under the eave in the back of the cabin. The squirrels had been getting in through it.

We brought our big generator that we had recently purchased and the Shop Vac, and I vacuumed downstairs. Upstairs, the squirrels had torn out the insulation on part of a wall that didn't have wood covering it yet. I threw away the messy plastic on the bed, picking up all the insulation pieces. The whole area needed to be vacuumed. I discovered a lot of squirrel poop in the corner, so I made a shopping list: we needed a large sheet of plastic, rubber gloves to fit me, more Lysol, and a mask to cover my nose and mouth.

So we drove to Walmart in Tell City. We each took half the list and split up. John bet me he'd get finished with his half of the list first. I hurried to find the stuff from my half of the list.

He showed up right when I completed my part. He was finished too, walking really fast toward the front, then slowing down when he realized he was way ahead. I suddenly ran and got ahead of him. He ran too. We passed a lady, laughing all the way. She giggled. We actually tied. Oh well.

Driving back to the cabin, we finished the work.

Then we walked over to look at Dry Lake. So peaceful. Then Nina showed up on her four-wheeler and JD's boat, trying to back it up to the lake. John tried to direct her when to turn. She finally did, and we helped her lift the boat into the lake.

Strolling down the lane, which looked like it had recently been re-rocked, I glanced down, seeing a large piece of an arrowhead laying in the rocks where we were about to step. I picked up the Indian relic, so excited to find another piece of history from this area! It was made of a light gray flint with some yellow/brown coloring running through it, and the point and the base of the arrowhead were broken off. I wish I knew more about it. I do know that it was a lot different shape and colors than the arrowhead I found on our lane.

We drove back to Sycamore Springs, leaving the next day.

We decided to drive to Tell City to buy a fire extinguisher, since we'll need a fire all night in our wood stove. As we pulled away from our property, we saw a lone deer crossing a meadow.

"I'll see you in the morning," John told it.

When we returned from town, the woods and yard were so bleak-looking in the dark. I'm glad I'm not alone, I thought. The night was really quiet.

"The dogs aren't barking," I said.

"Shhh, don't jinx us," John said. "I hear a car on the road. At home I wouldn't have noticed; there's so many."

The next morning he rose before dawn to hunt. When I got up later, I fed the fire first, then made myself a cup of coffee on the propane stove. Opening the curtains, I could see our woods and the meadow next door. The little tree, right outside our window, was covered with red berries shaped sort of like stars. The sky was overcast that morning. A hawk soared across the meadow, then circled the cabin, screeching. Oh, it's a red tailed hawk, I thought. I was glad to see a blue jay in the woods--a few years ago they had all died of West Nile disease.

Stepping outside to get another piece of wood for the fire, I heard a crow caw, a cow moo, and birds twittering in the woods. The trees were almost bare, except for a few brown leaves clinging, some green honey suckle, and the cedar trees dotting the woods.

When John walked down for us to go to the Hunter's Lunch at the church at Bristow; he said when he first climbed into his deer stand, a buck moved away before he had a chance to shoot it. Then once he stood up to stretch, he scared a doe away.

The lunch was great. Everything was homemade, and there was a big selection. The ladies from the church were bustling around, bringing in more food, and replenishing the coffee.

We sat with the Pastor, a man from Kentucky, and a young man with two children. He said he had lived at Elberfeld for two years and rented property from

Norbert _____. That morning his bathroom floor fell in and the Pastor and the man from Kentucky had repaired it.

"That was really nice of them to help you out," I remarked.

He nodded.

Afterwards, the Pastor took us to see his family's new house. It was really nice.

Returning to the cabin, John hunted some more, and I hung a couple of pictures and a towel rack. I put fresh sheets on the bed, replacing the plastic sheet on top.

A couple of days later we returned. I worked in the yard, picking up branches and cutting greenbriers. I rehung the hot pads and utensils in the cabin.

John built a fire in the stove, and we lit every candle and kerosene lantern in the place--so cozy. Once we stepped outside to view the full orange moon slipping up behind the frilly cedars and woods.

We hadn't noticed at first when we arrived at the cabin, but later when we walked out back, we could see the downed tree on the ground next to the outhouse with a huge branch laying across it. One side of the outhouse was broken; the door was ripped off and thrown into the pond!

John went to work with his chain saw, ending up with a couple of stacks of firewood. He braced up the side of the outhouse with a two by four and board he had (making do), and I tacked an old shower curtain temporarily across the outhouse opening.

When we visited JD, we were amazed that he had added a large living room/dining room onto his house. There were a lot of new windows on the side of the house facing Dry Lake, and a dining room table, a couple of big easy chairs, and a big comfortable couch. A painting was hanging on the wall of a lot of little bushes. He said he bought it from an artist in New Mexico.

We climbed up the new wrought iron spiral steps leading to a tower room, and there was a wonderful view of the lake! JD said he loved to sit up there and write.

Cabin Interior

8 NEW FRIENDS

We first met Bob when we were building our cabin. We turned around, and he was strolling toward us. He was tall. He said something like, I heard the hammering, so I thought I'd come over to find out what's going on. His cabin was down the road and up a lane. He and John talked awhile.

Then we stopped to see Katy. She wasn't doing too well and had decided to sell her place. Her mother was worried sick about her living out there by herself, and I was concerned about her too. She invited us in. John decided to go pack up our equipment, letting us women talk. She had the place fixed up really cute. I wished she wasn't moving. I liked her.

Tom was across the road working on that old trailer. The guy who was renting it moved out. He said they were going to burn up the old trailer and replace it with a new one--his brother was getting a divorce and moving there. It's next to the lane that leads to Dry Lake.

Nina, who had been visiting JD, had taken a plane to Oklahoma to meet her girlfriends for an outing. When we visited JD, the hummingbirds were swarming over his porch. Soon he's planning to drive to New Mexico to the other house he bought. He wants to live there in the winter, here in the summer.

Someone had told us Bob had drilled a well, so we went to visit him to ask him who he'd hired to drill it. We drove up his curvy lane through the woods, noticing a small cabin on the right, and wondering who lived there. Further up the lane, we admired a garden with green tomatoes hanging on the bushes surrounded by a fence. The scene was completed with a homemade scarecrow and some whirligigs like you might win at a fair.

A flock of colorful free range chickens ran from under the cabin, pecking around the steps; the roosters were a rich red brown color. Bob's cabin was twice as big as ours, I thought. It had a front door and a back door; what a view it must have with all the woods around! I liked his cabin immediately, but apparently no one was at home.

On the way out, we startled two fawns hiding in the tall weeds by the road. They looked warily at us. John said their mother was probably hiding behind the weeds, yelling "Didn't I tell you not to stand by the road? I know that guy. My mother told me about him. He's the dude that shot my dad." (John's a deer hunter).

Later we drove up to Bob's again, and he was at home. He and John had a good man to man conversation while I shot photos of the trees and chickens. The garden we had seen the last time on our way up here belonged to him.

I told Bob about how I was making so much racket in the cabin, but the deer were walking past the windows. It seemed like they were wondering what I was doing. I thought they'd be afraid to come around.

"The deer always come by when I'm making a lot of noise," he said. "I think they're just nosy."

"They know you're doing something and aren't hunting for them," John said.

After that we kept hearing a machine roaring and hammering coming from that direction, but we were so busy, we didn't make it up there to find out what was happening.

When we were looking at Girly Creek, we could see someone across the thin wooded area at that little cabin that we had noticed when we were driving up Bob's lane. The cedar trees were sprinkled here and there. We walked over to introduce ourselves, and he said his name was Richard.

"My wife's in a wheelchair now, so we haven't been making it here much anymore," he said.

"We're glad we happened to meet you," John said. I smiled, nodding in agreement.

"Used to, we were here a lot, so now once in a while I get to missing this place. Would you all like a cup of coffee? I just made a pot." He took us inside the cabin, opening a cabinet door for two more cups, and filling them from the pot. Walking back outside, we stood around, sipping coffee.

It was a cute little cabin. It was painted red and was their get-away cabin. It was probably about the size of ours but didn't have an upstairs.

"I like your cabin," I commented.

"Thanks. It's just the right size for two people. I hire someone to mow my property once a year, so it doesn't turn into a thicket," he said.

"That's good. We're letting most of our property grow into a woods. We like a lot of wildlife," John said.

"Would it be okay if I gathered a few rocks from the creek?"

"Sure, that would be fine," John answered. The creek was running across our property. I can't recall what else we discussed, but we thought he was a nice person.

Our grandson, Mikey came over to our house, spending the night. The next day he went with us to look at Katy's house for sale next to our cabin. We were thinking that if we bought her house, and it adjoined our property, we could use the cabin as an office and art and photography studio for our desks and hobbies. The realtor was there. Her house was fixed up really nice.

"I've left some of my nicer furniture, so it would look good when prospective buyers came. I left some furniture in the bedroom too. Look in there. Does it look okay?" she asked.

"It looks great!" I answered after I looked.

"I'm moving into an apartment in a small town," she said. "Some of my furniture is already there."

She told us the price they wanted for her house, and it was reasonable. We asked the realtor if we could sell our house, so we could buy this one.

"No," he said. "We can't wait that long. We need to sell it right away."

And we knew this was true. Katy couldn't wait around. She had her apartment, and needed to sell the house as soon as possible.

We took Mikey to our cabin and later we walked over to the lake to hike around. He loved the beach.

It wasn't long after that when Katy's house sold. I missed her. We hoped she was doing o.k. I wondered who bought her house.

We looked at a house for sale overlooking Dry Lake. I don't remember a whole lot about it, but it was a modular home. The price was rather high, I thought. Its main good feature, in my opinion, was that it was next to Dry Lake. Later we found that the owner didn't have access to the lake because it was not one of the properties sold by the farmer who owned the lake.

We had come to the cabin a few times lately. John had been working on his deer stands and set up a photo blind in our woods, so he can take photos of deer.

We walked up the hill together to look at it. Our woods was so pretty, it was full of oak trees, and the forest floor was carpeted with leaves. The trees were so colorful then (October), I was thinking to myself.

On the property below the cabin we discovered a couple of larger cypress trees we didn't realize had survived. We had planted the trees years ago.

Walking on the lane over to Dry Lake, we saw a lot of deer tracks along the way. Having heard it had been drained, we wanted to check it out. Someone said they had removed the plug from the spillway. Apparently they were trying to keep the lake water out of people's property and from flooding over the road as we've heard it does sometimes.

The lake seemed okay; of course the water was lower, but it was still beautiful! A couple was fishing, and she pulled a string of large catfish out of the water to show us. They told us how he had lost his rod in the lake, and she had paddled out in a paddle boat to retrieve it. They were friends of a guy who just bought the small building by the lake.

Around that time we heard that Randy's wife was killed in a car accident. He wasn't interested in coming to their trailer by himself. We haven't seen him since.

When we were at the cabin, we walked up the lane to see Bob, and he introduced us to Shelly, a woman he met from out west who was visiting him. They were working on his big new log cabin. That explained all the new noises we had been hearing!

She showed me the inside of Bob's old cabin. The original main room had kitchen cabinets with mismatched doors, a table and chairs, a couch, and a plastic sink. She told me that there was also a little loft, and that he had added two rooms. I really liked it--it looked like a cozy place.

Their break was over, and they resumed working, so we walked along Fossil Creek all the way to the end. We passed The Swimming Hole and the place where we had found the wild irises. Coming out on the Four-Wheeler Road, we hiked back, hearing coyotes howling in the distance, and a barred owl.

We noticed that the squirrels had returned, as we were walking up our driveway, chewing holes in three corner soffits of our cabin! After entering, we climbed the ladder, finding a nest in our bedroom again. There were two squirrels outside chasing each other through the branches of the big oak tree.

When we drove into our lane, we realized that the new people must have moved into Katy's house. There was a different vehicle parked in the driveway.

Our new next door neighbor's dog barked all evening. About the same time we went to bed, the people came home. Their big loud hunting dog had barked until midnight when John made up his mind to walk over to their house, complaining that we couldn't sleep because of their dog! What an unusual way to meet a new neighbor! The dog was pretty quiet after that.

John told me that the new neighbor's name was Trent; he seemed like a nice guy.

The next morning when we were drinking coffee by the wood stove, we saw a deer cross the field two times. Then the dogs next door barked, and it and three other deer hopped away, their white tails flagging.

Driving to Tell City, we bought lamp oil and propane. When we returned John wanted to hike down the creek, which was full of water. My boots were at home, so I didn't go along. While he was out, he ran into Bob, Shelly, and Reggie, who I hadn't met yet. John said that Reggie said he stayed in a shack nearby.

Then John hunted, but he didn't see any deer.

We finally went to the cabin. After lunch we visited Shelly and Bob. Their cabin was really coming along. They told us that JD sold his house, and was moving permanently to his other house in New Mexico. We were surprised! He hadn't told us he was selling it, and we usually don't drive by his place on the way to the cabin, so we hadn't seen a For Sale sign. I wondered where Nina was. Shelly said they had met the people who bought his house, and they seemed nice.

The redbuds and dogwoods and phlox were blooming. I saw a large rabbit (Thumper?) run out of a thicket behind the cabin, and a flycatcher perched on a branch.

We camped at Sycamore Springs. We liked to go there for a change of pace--we have met a lot of campers, and the Little Blue River runs through it. A lady we had met years ago was riding her motorized wheelchair around the drive circling the campers. She stopped to talk to us.

"This is our last camping trip," Maggie said.

"Why? What's wrong?" we asked. She and her husband had been camping there for years, usually for a week at a time. They were the first fellow campers we met!

"We're both in bad shape. Earl fell off the porch, banging himself all up; and I'm having trouble breathing, so it's time to quit," she said. She was so sad to have to give it up.

We said our good-byes--I about cried. When she rode away I remembered all the fun times we had. I especially think of the time we left some stuff laying on the picnic table while we took our showers at the camp bathrooms. When we returned, our things had been rifled through. We noticed our knife was missing. Then John saw a raccoon running away.

When Maggie came by, we told her about the knife and raccoon. "I can just imagine the raccoon walking around to each camp, holding up the knife and saying, "Your cookies or your life!!" she said. We all laughed. She always had this effect on us.

Driving around on our way to the cabin, we looked at a trailer for sale in Branchville. Not that we were particularly interested in the trailer, but there was a natural spring flowing out of the hills that provided its water supply. There was a creek running on the other side of the road, and the interesting little town around it.

At the cabin, I was admiring the lovely purple wildflowers blooming, or maybe they were blue--they were either Venus looking-glass or tall bellflowers, I wasn't sure. John walked up to his hunting spot, and I beachcombed in the creek. When John came down, we drove up to visit Bob and Shelly. They were preparing to go out to eat pizza and beer. We showed them my children's book, *We're Combing the Beaches and Doing Projects* that was recently published. Shelly said she saw me when I was interviewed on TV.

We visited with our new neighbors, Trent and Amy. They didn't have their big hunting dog anymore.

A For Sale sign was posted on Randy's property--it was being sold by a realtor. We walked over to the lake, discovering that they had drained it again! All kinds of birds--herons, egrets, geese--were catching fish. It was a beautiful scene! A neighbor's friendly dog decided to walk with us, and we hiked on a trail past the little camper that was parked by the lake--it was in bad shape. Vandals won't leave it alone! Some people were fishing, so we introduced ourselves. It turned out that they were the owners of the camper and that property. All these years we had been walking over there, and we finally met them! I'm glad there were such nice people around. John, the dog, and I walked around the trail to the other exit to the road.

There we met a man in a red car, driving slowly. He asked us about a lake and property for sale, so John pointed to Randy's property. After he looked at it, he told us he had written a book about how to take care of yourself--organic food and exercise and yoga.

We walked him over to the lake, and he thought it was beautiful too! I don't believe I've ever seen it when it wasn't. He asked about a boat chained to a tree that had bullet holes in it, and we said that happened to the old boat we owned too. When it disappeared, we knew that we could never leave our canoes chained up by the lake!

It seems to be a rule that nothing is all good or nothing is perfect. For example, sometimes it seems that The Land is wonderful! There are wildflowers, a pretty creek, birds, red hills, and a lake--then someone shoots up your boat or a dog tries to bite you. For as soon as a person begins to think that it is paradise, something has to happen.

John offered to show him our cabin, and he wanted to see it. He said he liked it much better than the house trailer, and he was interested in buying it!

"Trent wants to buy it too," John said. I was surprised!

"I don't want to sell it," I said. John gave him our business card.

Driving back to Sycamore Springs, I prepared supper, and we ate it by the picnic table. The next day, we took a scenic drive through Leavenworth and ended up at Stagecoach Campground by the Blue River. The gate was locked, so we drove around finding another way to a beach by climbing down some large tree roots. It wasn't the beach we usually were on, but I beach combed and John fly fished. I found another curved flint artifact, probably made of Indiana hornstone. I hope that the Stagecoach Campground gate isn't permanently locked!

We moved on to Corydon, which at one time was Indiana's state capital, eating a picnic lunch we brought with us at the town square park. Watching people walking by and doing their thing is always interesting. Why are those little boys running away from their mother? Why was that woman wearing a patterned purple shirt with blue striped shorts?

Afterwards we looked around at the Red Barn antique shop, a favorite place of ours. We always seemed to see something we liked, but not much that we bought. Then we went to a consignment shop, the Goodwill, and the Salvation Army.

We drove to the library in English to check our email. I heard from my publisher that there will be a book signing for ten local authors, counting me if I wanted. I wrote back to include me. It was to be at Central Library in Evansville, November 9th. Then we headed to the campground for supper by our campfire.

The next day we met Carol who had a small vintage camper about the size of ours. She asked us to look inside--it was lovely!

We packed up. Then we drove toward home on the scenic route, stopping to eat a picnic lunch at Grandview overlooking the Ohio River, and then to a little thrift shop at Rockport before we headed for home.

Another day Bob and Shelly were planning to visit us at the cabin. We had just arrived, so I hurriedly swept the floor--it was covered with dead bugs. When I visited the outhouse I found a bird's nest on the little shelf meant to hold the toilet paper, and laying in the nest was a white egg.

In the cabin, we sat on the Adirondack couch

and some chairs, visiting. Then the four of us hiked through Bob's property, which I think he said was 60 acres, plus we walked through the state forest. There were daffodils blooming in the woods, and a big dry creek was running through the property. I loved hiking in all that space!

John shot a photo of Bob, Shelly, and me holding hands around a big tree. I took a picture of John, Bob, and Shelly casually leaning on a big vine that hung between two trees. It was a lot of fun, good exercise, and a good place to bond with friends for two or three hours. Then we walked to their cabin for iced tea.

When we arrived at the cabin, we carried in all our stuff and changed the bedding (a mouse had made a nest); then walking up their lane taking our kerosene lantern with us, we visited Shelly and Bob. Their cabin was beautifully furnished and had electricity and water. Shelly decorated it with her Indian baskets and ivory figures. They planned to work on the basement next. We sat around in their comfortable living room, talking about politics (us) and about hunting (the guys). Right before we left, Bob was telling us about the mountain lion he thought he saw. I had never heard of any living in Indiana.

We said our good byes and began walking down their lane after lighting the lantern. I kept hearing scary noises in the woods, like an animal sneaking around--a mountain lion? The woods were dark, impenetrable.

Upon approaching the road, we heard scuttling sounds, like feet running.

"Must be deer," John said. There was a light in front of Tammy's house. John looked that way.

"It wasn't deer!" he exclaimed. They've TPed Tammy's tree!"

Looking at the tree, in the misty light I could see white strips flying around. Up the road a light flashed on, and then we heard a motor start. I saw long shadows on the road, and people scurrying around. We were standing there looking at the tree. "She'll think we did it if she sees us out here," I commented.

A couple of dogs were looking at us as we walked down the road. One jumped up on John. "I know you," John said. The other dog looked at me.

"I know you too," I said. So they followed us back to the cabin.

I didn't think there were mountain lions in Indiana; however, later I saw an article in the paper where one had been caught on film in Indiana (it wasn't close to there, though). I've heard if you encounter a mountain lion, don't make eye contact, lean over, approach it, or run, but if you're attacked, fight back. I also read that a bear was seen near Corydon, IN.

The next day Bob and Shelly came to see us. Sitting by our cozy wood stove fire, we talked. They asked us to go with them to visit their friend, Sam.

So we followed them to Sam's place. We passed his lane every time we came to the cabin, but of course we didn't know him yet then. He lived in an earth sheltered cabin that he had built himself. The hill rose up to the cabin roof on the back, and two sides. It was like one big room inside, heated with a wood stove with a flat rock wall behind it. It was really full, lined with books. Sam was a lot like us--he said he liked the feel of a real book in his hands, not an electronic device. There was a gas refrigerator and stove, no electricity, with a little bathroom tacked on as an after-thought.

We liked the bottle tree in his front yard, which had colorful bottles stuck down over branches all over it and the pond in the front yard. He raised chickens too. Sam was really nice and talked about the possibility of his girlfriend moving in too.

9 SPENDING TIME AT THE CABIN

John and I were on our way to the cabin, stopping to eat at Wendy's near Ferdinand when we ran into Laura, who worked at the same print shop I did about 25 years ago. She was with her husband--they had dated for 10 years before they married. I said John and I dated for about two months before we married.

Laura and I talked about our troubles with the print shop owner's wife. I told her how I'd walked out one day, and that woman chased me down the street begging me to return.

"Why didn't you come talk to me about it?" she had asked me.

"You're not approachable," I answered.

We remembered the time the pressmen set a life size cardboard man in front of the open bathroom door in the basement, turning out all the lights, possibly to scare Laura or Pat. Oh course I didn't know about it, so I walked through the dark basement, reaching into the bathroom to turn on the light. Eeeeeeeeek!!! A tall man was standing in front of me!! Then I realized what happened—and I knew that the pressmen would tease me forever, so I calmed down before walking back past them. Apparently they hadn't heard me scream over their loud presses, so they never knew.

It was so good to see Laura again. We agree to be friends on Facebook so we could keep in touch.

We arrived at the cabin late. John built a fire, setting a big chunk of oak in the stove for the night, before we went to bed.

John got up about 5:00 a.m. to go hunting; and when I rose later, I added wood to the fire, lighting the propane stove to heat up my coffee water. While sipping my coffee, I observed the view through the south windows. It was a wet day, but the rain had stopped. The bare trees wore shiny droplets of water like iridescent Christmas ornaments. Green lichens mottled their trunks, and the field behind was a yellow ochre and light rust color. A bird was diving into the grasses for breakfast, I guessed. Of course the green cedar trees and white tree trunks sticking up finished the lovely scene.

I hated to leave this pretty view, but the outhouse was calling me, so I quickly dressed.

After eating oatmeal and coffee for breakfast, I installed three blinds we had bought in a thrift shop, feeding the wood stove on breaks.

John didn't get a deer, so we drove home.

We returned to the cabin after church the next day to pick up the utility trailer. John decided to hunt as it was the last day for gun season.

While he hunted, I walked around the creek with my camera. I could see Bob and Shelly's cabin across the creek from in front of Randy's trailer. As I strolled back on the lane, I saw two birds land in a cedar tree. I stood quietly, watching until I got a glimpse of one of them--a Rufus-sided towhee. I believe the partially hidden brownish bird was its mate.

The sun was setting, and the sky was pink as I entered the cabin. I played with my camera inside, shooting through the windows, and at the furniture.

Finally I heard a noise outside and thought that John was approaching. I didn't see him out the window, but the two gray squirrels were chasing each other through the branches in the dusk. I had lit the kerosene lamp, and the flame was dancing around like a crazed mouse twirling a lit match! I sat waiting for him, my mind ticking off all the things that could have happened: he had hypothermia and couldn't move, he fell out of the stand and broke his leg, or a wild hog mauled him.

As I sat there I thought I heard the faraway quack of a duck. It must be flying to the lake. I was biting my nails when I heard the neighbor's dogs barking, and I jumped up to look out the window. A light shone in the dark woods, moving down the hill toward me. Soon he was stepping in the door, into my arms!

Before Christmas we decided we didn't want to buy a Christmas tree or use our old artificial tree. I wanted a real tree from The Land, but I didn't want to cut down one of our few precious pine trees. We decided to cut one of the many cedar trees.

So we drove to the cabin, picking a cedar tree that was growing too close to another tree and could never grow straight. John cut it down. He probably thought it was too tall, so he cut some off the bottom. It was like you may have read in a story book: They all dressed in their warmest coats, walking out of the cabin into the woods to pick out a Christmas tree! We did that too.

At home, after we strung the lights onto the cedar tree, we decorated it with mostly homemade ornaments. We hung the cabin ornaments Shirley had painted when she was around eight or nine years old and that our other kids and grandkids had painted, setting the star on top that Jessica made when she was a teenager. I found the hand-turned wooden ornaments that my dad made after he retired--Santa, horses, soldiers, a clown-- and hung them. I've always loved them all!

John and I brought the two white enameled metal cabinets to the cabin that we purchased at half price at a thrift store. One we carried upstairs, so we could keep our extra bedding safe. The other one we worked into the kitchen area to hold food and dishes.

Taking a break, we visited Shelly and Bob, sitting in the four Adirondack chairs on their front porch. We could still see Bob's original small cabin, but to me it added another dimension to the place--then and now.

I loved the view of the woods in every direction we could see! I pointed to an indigo bunting in the trees--a beautiful blue bird. Then a summer tanager, a scarlet bird, delighted us by perching in the tree right in front of us. I've never seen one at home. Their chickens strolled by. One of them tried to peck a potted plant on the porch, so Bob shooed it away.

When we were ready to get back to work, Shelly and I walked through their cabin as John and Bob walked to the edge of the porch, ready to jump off. There were no steps down to the ground yet, so there was a big drop off. When we came out the kitchen door, John was lying on the ground below the porch wearing a pained look on his face, like he fell off! But I detected a grin, and then we all were laughing!

Another day when we all sat out on their porch, it was becoming dark. Shelly carried each of the younger chickens to the garage for the night, one by one. She explained it was because the older chickens picked on them.

We passed a bunch of guys dressed in camo, talking loudly, and laughing as we arrived at the cabin. Their campers were parked in a formerly empty space next to the house trailer across the road.

It soon was dark, so we climbed into bed early. It was really cold upstairs. John placed a big piece of oak wood in the wood stove, but it didn't heat the upstairs all that much. We piled all the blankets we had on the bed.

At 5:30 a.m. John woke up, dressed; and after adding more wood to the stove, he left to hunt. I couldn't go back to sleep--it was too cold!

Right away I got up--I was freezing up there without John, my furnace! I climbed the ladder downstairs, huddled under a blanket in a plastic lounge chair by the wood stove, while heating water on the propane stove for coffee.

Later I boiled water on the wood stove, so I could wash dishes. Then John called me saying he shot two deer. He didn't know yet if they were dead until he followed their trails (I'm so thankful we can finally use our cell phones up here). He walked down to the cabin to fetch the sled and rope, and I decided to make fish chowder for lunch. After a time, he climbed down the hill, pulling the sled with a deer in it. Then later he brought the other deer.

Bob and Shelly had seen John pulling a couple a deer he had shot. I hadn't seen him yet because I was busy cooking the soup. They came to the cabin with him, and the place looked like a cyclone had hit it! There was hunting equipment all over the place! Shelly spotted the lounge chair with the wadded up blanket and pillow on it.

"Did you sleep on the lounge chair last night?" she asked.

"My furnace got up at 5:30 this morning to go hunting, and I was cold, so I came down here to sleep," I answered.

She smiled. Then Bob noticed the lounge chair with the blanket on it and asked the same thing. Shelly told him what I just said to her.

I had swept the cabin and John had cut down the small trees that were close around the cabin. We reasoned that the squirrels couldn't get in if there weren't any close trees for them to climb up, but we wondered if they could go to the very end of the branch of the huge oak tree on the hill and jump to the cabin roof. There's no way we could cut that tree down. It would definitely be too dangerous, and it would be our luck if we did--it would fall on the cabin! It would cost a fortune to have it cut down, even if someone was able to do it!

We visited Bob and Shelly for about 15 minutes, returning to the cabin because John wanted to watch that humungous tree to see if the squirrels were still around. We hadn't seen them recently. John said that maybe they're already dead or moved on. He thought this because I had found a squirrel skeleton when I was moving the furniture around.

The next time we came to the cabin, we hiked with Shelly and Bob behind our cabin and up the hill. The guys were talking, and I remember Shelly telling me about some antique clothes she had that belonged to her grandmother. They were beautiful and in good condition, hanging in her closet; however, it would be nice if they were displayed where people could view them.

We were walking in the Hoosier National Forest when we looked across the fence at a farm. Then we walked to Two Deer Ridge.

When we returned, we talked to Trent and he told us Amy just had a baby girl. After our congratulations, I noticed the sun was shining on Girly Creek, and I thought it looked so beautiful. As always, I was enjoying the calming sounds it made. The guys were talking, and Shelly and I discussed politics and the possibility of participating in a yard sale along Hwy. 66 that went on for miles.

Afterwards, we drove to Ferdinand for a late lunch. On the way to Jasper, we drove past the YMCA and the library. We had been wondering where they were located.

John has always wanted to buy the meadow plus the three acres of woods next to our property, mainly because we wouldn't want anyone to build a house right beside us like it was in town. It would also give us a place so we could have a garden, John would have more space to hunt, and we could probably build a cistern because of the excess water running down the hill. We had talked to the owner before, and his price was too much. So John called him again, and because they really wanted to sell it, they reduced their price.

We met Danny and his wife, Bea, at the court house to buy their property. This was the first time we met his wife. Immediately, we discovered that they needed a legal deed before we could do anything! With the help of the ladies at the court house, we found a lawyer for them and were driving to his office.

The lawyer's receptionist said it would take 1-1 ½ hours to take care of it, so we all ate breakfast together at a café. Afterwards, we looked around an antique store until she called, saying it was ready. Then we signed everything, giving our neighbors the check. We drove back to the court house so we could finish. Our previous neighbors were nice people. Too bad we hadn't known them years ago.

We now owned eight acres. We'll need to hire someone with a tractor to cut the front acre once a year like Danny did, so it will continue to be a meadow.

I planted several rose of Sharon trees and John planted five different plants that his daughter sent us for Christmas, including huckleberry and raspberry off to the side of the new property. Then John sawed up the little trees we had cut down from around the cabin, stacking them for firewood, and with the branches I made a thicket for the rabbit to hide in. It's hard to be a rabbit around there because there's so many predators.

When we pulled into the lane to our cabin, we noticed Bob and Trent were driving their four-wheelers down the road. After we parked our truck, they drove into our lane. When I looked, I saw they had parked their vehicles in our driveway, each sitting on his four-wheeler seat. Trent's little boy was sitting in the rocks, playing. His housedog, Dixie, was sitting nearby. John walked down and stood with his arms folded across his chest, talking with them. This was the way men visited.

After we took the stuff we brought into the cabin, we crossed the creek, hopping from rock to rock at the place where West Fork and Girly Creek joined, to the other side of the creek, and up the hill to Bob and Shelly's cabin. We visited for a little while, then we all decided to take a hike through our new property. Besides the acre that is a meadow next to our cabin, behind and up the hill is a lot of woods. It was a good hike.

Afterwards John spread the black plastic to kill weeds where he planned for the garden to be on the new property. He gathered large rocks from the creek to hold it down.

John and I took the white Hoosier cabinet we bought to the cabin. I had fallen in love with it when we saw it in the shop, and John liked it too. We bought it at a good price--we had seen others that were more than four times the price of ours. John also had the chest of drawers he bought a few years ago that had been in our garage. Bob and Shelly came over, and John and Bob carried the two pieces of furniture into the cabin, taking out the things we wanted to replace.

Then we all walked up to Reggie's. He had some land nearby with a couple of small buildings. I liked the way he planted daffodils and crocuses along the edge of the woods. He was getting ready to build a pole barn and plans to move here from Chicago. They said another guy is moving into the cabin that Richard and his wife used to own by the lane to Bob's cabin.

John noticed that the Clariton Motel in Evansville was closing, and they were selling furniture, appliances, and miscellaneous stuff. John and I explored the whole thing. Never having walked around in an almost empty, large motel before, this was quite an experience! We bought a large bathroom sink, a black apartment size fridge, and a stand that holds the fridge and a microwave oven for the cabin.

At Harbor Freight, John was looking at some ramps that were on sale. He was thinking about buying them to connect our two Grumman canoes together, making a Catamaran to float in Dry Lake. He decided they were too thin and short.

We drove to Rural King to take a class on how to raise chickens; it was taught by a young woman. It was very complicated, I thought, and there were a lot of equipment, medicines, and vitamins to buy.

She said to discipline a rooster if he attacks someone, hold him upside down by his feet in front of the hens. It embarrasses him. She said, if that's not enough, dunk him quickly in water. The person he attacks has to do this.

According to her, the reason to raise chickens isn't to save money, but to know what you're eating. Nothing is better than a fresh chicken egg. John won a $5 coupon and I won a watering bucket for chickens that was worth $20. We came out unsure if we ever wanted to raise chickens.

We met the man, again after all these years, from the gas and electric company. He said it would cost about $3,000.00 for us to have electricity, or we could make monthly payments if we lived on the property. We would also have to pay someone to dig a trench along the driveway. John said maybe we should look into solar.

Bob and Shelly planned to attend a couple of events around the area, and they invited us to go along too. First we drove to Derby for the 6th Annual Steel Guitar get-together. The musicians sang and played their instruments very well.

Then we drove on to Tell City where there was a summer picnic at a church. There were a lot of booths which were spread out on the courthouse lawn, and just about anything you could want was for sale. Shelly line danced with her group. We ate lunch, buying freshly cooked hamburgers off the grill of one of the vendors, visiting, and watching all the people milling around. There was a lively raffle in progress. Afterwards John bought a strawberry rhubarb pie to take home. He always did have a sweet tooth.

Back at the cabin, the butterfly weeds were blooming in what is now our new meadow, covered with all kinds of orange and brown butterflies. What a beautiful sight!

After we drove to Louisville, KY to pick up the dulcimer we bought on eBay, on our return trip we stopped at the cabin to drop off the furniture we had bought at the motel sale. All the new stuff was filling the cabin, so we'll have to return to rearrange everything. I readied the Amish table to take to my granddaughter if she wants it.

Then we stopped by for a quick visit with Shelly

and Bob. They have the most beautiful cat with a big fluffy tail. He usually hides when we visit. John brought his handgun to show to Bob, and we all wanted to hold it, trying to aim it.

John planted a sweet potato patch on our new property, gathering more rocks to hold the plastic in place. We used the creek water to wash our hands, water the plants, and clean the shovel. I was glad water was flowing in the creek.

At home the next day, John couldn't find his handgun. He called Shelly to ask if he left it on their couch, but she couldn't find it. So he asked Bob if he would look out by the potato patch in case he dropped it, but he didn't see it either.

The next day we were back at the cabin, looking for John's handgun. I looked around the driveway, and he searched around the garden. He found it!

We saw the cutest little baby raccoon climbing a tree in Trent's yard. We talked to Trent and Amy, and they said we could hook up our electricity by digging along the lane if we decided we want it.

Back at the cabin, I rearranged the furniture to fit in the Hoosier cabinet, the sink, the stand holding the little refrigerator, and the chest of drawers. I thought it looked a lot better.

I planted Easter flowers along the trees by the driveway. Okay Reggie, I'm a copycat, I thought to myself. Next, I planned a circular flower bed on the new property, so we can see it from the cabin. After I placed the rocks in a circle, I planted some tall pink phlox, known to attract butterflies, that I brought from home. Soon I plan to plant a butterfly bush that Shirley is giving us. John checked on the sweet potato patch.

On the way home we each ate a hot fudge sundae at McDonalds while watching news on their big screen TV. You can tell we like to rough it every chance we can.

Shelly wrote saying her friend Susan and her husband Cory were visiting, and she wanted us to meet them. When we arrived, Shelly was ready to leave for work; so we sat on the front porch with Bob and Shelly's friends, getting to know each other. They had lived in a sail boat in Olympia, Washington for seven years. They lived right by the town.

They had recently bought the 21 foot motor home that they drove down here. Susan said it had more room than the boat. They had a dog, an Australian shepherd, who was very shy. Susan said they had visited Shelly and Bob before they built the new cabin, and they helped work on the cabin each time they returned. She and John had their love of photography in common.

We returned to their log cabin so John and Susan could talk photography. Shelly's chickens were sick, so she drove to Tell City to buy them medicine. Bob and Cory were working on the cabin. One of the things they did while they were visiting was build steps up to the front porch! It was so wonderful to be able to just walk up the stairs to the porch. I know Shelly was happy.

Ben flew home from California for about a week, and we were so glad to see him. He was wanting to hunt at The Land while he was here, so we spent a few days at the cabin. Ben slept on a cot downstairs at night. The guys hiked up to the woods to check out John's deer stands. John spent some time shooting photos. We brought the trail camera to check upstairs to see if we still had squirrels.

I had filled large jugs with water, freezing them in our freezer at home, so we could use our new refrigerator like an old time ice box. Setting three jugs in the fridge, I was able to put our milk, cans of diet root beer, mustard, jelly, etc. in the ice box, keeping everything cold! My sister remembers when our family had an ice box when she was little, and ice was delivered to the house. I guess by the time I came along, they had quit doing that. We haven't brought a microwave because I can't think of any way we could use it except with a generator, and it wouldn't be worth it to me.

While the guys hunted, I puttered in the cabin doing all the things I've been wanting to do and warmed the pot of venison stew. All the stew eventually disappeared.

One night we ate at Marcy's in Leopold. For dessert Ben and I shared a chocolate/ice cream dessert! It was so-o-o good! We drove to Tell City to a gun shop, and John asked me not to let him buy another gun. I was browsing around; when I looked up, he was holding a rifle, aiming it, and asking the price!

"Hold it right there; you said to stop you," I said. One guy turned around, staring at me.

"You sound just like Kim _____," he said. "You look a lot like her too. You could be her mother!" I wasn't sure this was a compliment. How old was this woman, anyway?

"Does she live in Tell City?" I asked.

"Yes. She's a mile carrier," it sounded like he said. He had an accent; he meant mail carrier.

John bought some shells for his rifle, and Ben bought a case for the handgun his grandma gave him. Ben gave me a case he had for my handgun.

Sunday, while the guys were in the woods hunting, I drove to Michael's to buy lunch. I really enjoyed the drive. It occurred to me that this was the first time I had driven to Michael's by myself. I saw the log house with the barn that was for sale. I passed the farm that I've always loved, and the black dog chased my car just like it usually does. I went by the driveway to Sam's place; I also saw the place with the big barn and lake that we considered buying years ago. The abandoned cabin was still standing on that corner after all these years.

At Michael's I looked at the cooked food for sale in the glass case. It was a familiar place. It's not actually called Michael's anymore, but it'll always be Michael's to us. The guys couldn't tell me what they wanted to eat; they were still in the woods when I left. John just called me on his cell phone, asking me to "pick up some lunch for us." I ordered them each a two piece chicken box, including potato logs, slaw, and a biscuit and a chicken salad sandwich for me.

Trent and Reggie each shot a deer. Someone across the road got one too, and there were a lot of cars and four wheelers cruising around like the circus had just come to town. I felt bad for the deer! I also missed the quiet atmosphere we usually had at the cabin.

John and I walked around in the woods, looking over the new three acres before we left, spotting an old property marker made of stone. He was happy to find a beech tree on our land.

Then we hurried off so we could make it home before dark.

John, Ben, and Ben's friend went to The Land another day to hunt, and I believe Ben and his friend went once again after that. Ben always did like The Land.

On Christmas day, we attended church in the morning, then we drove to the cabin to check it out. We looked at the SD card from our trail camera we left upstairs. There were photos of three gray squirrels, climbing all around! Oh no, they ARE back!!

Then we followed Bob and Shelly to Tell City to eat a buffet lunch at the Chinese restaurant. Another couple, friends of Shelly and Bob that we just met, joined us. The food was great, and we really enjoyed everyone's company!

I thought I had read about a product that could be purchased to repel pests such as mice, so I looked at a store, finding packages that could be stashed in drawers and cabinets to keep mice and other pesky animals away. Then I heard that moth balls can repel other pests besides moths. We bought some of each and the next time we were at the cabin, before leaving, we laid the repellent in the cabinet shelves and drawers. We also set small open containers of mothballs around, especially upstairs where the squirrels were probably entering. Then we left.

We will have to remove the mothballs when we return because they smell awful, and it couldn't be good to have them in the room with us.

The next couple of times we were at the cabin, we didn't find any evidence of mice or squirrels in our cabin. Maybe they're gone!

10 IT'S A TOSS UP

We considered selling the cabin because the taxes on the cabin had risen tremendously. If my memory serves me correctly, when we first bought our four acres, our taxes were $24.00 every six months. Of course we now have a small cabin on our property, but should our taxes have risen to close to 20 times that amount every six months? According to the paperwork, they were taxing us for a three bedroom home with a bathroom, furnace, running water, and electricity.

In our Appeal, I wrote them a long letter that we do not have any of those things. What we do have is a 16'x16' rustic cabin with a sleeping loft, using a ladder to climb upstairs. There is no foundation--it is built like a pole barn. We have no electricity or wiring. There is no well, no plumbing--no running water. There is no bathroom--no inside toilet or shower, no septic system.

We have no furnace, but we do have a wood stove. We have no mailing address and receive no mail there.

Apparently no one had even looked at our cabin before they taxed it. They adjusted it, but it was still a whole lot higher than it had been. It is a big burden because we already have our home taxes.

John and I had driven to some places along the Tradewater River in Western Kentucky. It is over 130 miles long and is a tributary of the Ohio River. John said we should move there because it's in the country and it's hilly.

"The Land is in the country and hilly," I pointed out.

John drew a plan for a 20'x24' addition to the cabin. It would be two stories high, standing on legs in the driveway below the original cabin. Downstairs would be the living room, kitchen, and dining room--all in one large room, heated with a masonry stove near the center. Upstairs would be the master bedroom, bathroom, and a photography/art studio. He said we could park our cars underneath it; and probably we could place the washer, dryer, and freezer as well as have a work area down there. There would be a deck from this building to the cabin, and we'd walk on the deck to the other part of the house! The cabin would be the spare bedroom with a storage room upstairs.

I would think the addition (plus a well, masonry stove, and electricity) would cost a lot more than we could possible make from selling our house. I wouldn't want to walk outside at night to get to the other part-- something might get me, and we may be too old to climb all those stairs all the time.

We stayed at the cabin for a couple of nights while John searched for water on the hill and ponds. He looked for a spring or run off place. He said the pond on the hill may have a little water. A man he met said he should dig down to bedrock and put a pump on it. Then we used the weed-eater on the driveway and around the cabin.

"I would like us to move to the cabin. I really would like to move to Oregon, but the cabin will do," John said.

"I really couldn't live in a cabin with this plan," I said.

As much as we love it, the cabin is the only thing we've ever disagreed about. I think it's because it means so much to both of us. So we came up with a couple of new ideas:

Plan 2, would be to attach the addition onto the south side of the cabin. On the main floor would be the living room, possibly smaller than the first plan, with a masonry stove near the center (we've always wanted one). The kitchen would be on one side. The dining room table, the living room furniture, and our desks would be arranged pleasingly in the rest of the room around the stove. Upstairs would be an art/photography studio, a bedroom, and a bathroom. The cabin would be a guest bedroom, and it would be heated by the existing wood stove; upstairs would be a storage area.

We would build a screened-in porch on the west side of the addition. Since the cabin and the addition are on a hill, there could be a garage dug under the addition, so we could drive up our driveway into the garage.

We both liked this plan, but even if we sold our house in Evansville, it might still be too expensive. It might be possible if we left off the upstairs, using the cabin for the bedroom. Also, I wouldn't like to lose all those windows along the south side of the cabin--the sun warms the cabin quite a bit.

Plan 3, we would build an addition (a lean-to) behind the cabin, turning the double window in the kitchen into a door between the two rooms. There wouldn't be as much ground space to build the lean-to as there would be in plan 2 because there is a hill and a woods behind it. Possibly we could cut into the hill, eliminating a few trees to enlarge it. The addition would be heated with a masonry stove, maybe in the middle or possibly set into the wall between the addition and the cabin, so it could heat both rooms. Then we would use the wood stove only when it was really cold in the winter. We might add a cellar to store root vegetables and as a safe place to go in case of a bad storm.

The original cabin would be our bedroom, and the upstairs would be a guest room/art and photography studio. The addition would be laid out similarly to plan 2, except it won't be quite as large, our desks might have to be in the bedroom or upstairs. We would add a bathroom on the north side of the cabin, by the bedroom, so we would have access to it from all places. Later on, we would add a screened in porch onto the south side.

We invited Bob and Shelly over to show them our sketched ideas in case we decided to add onto the cabin. They thought the sketches were cool. Afterwards Shelly had to go to work, so we looked at the lower part of our new property. There was a natural ditch full of water running down the hill. We think that may be where we should dig a well.

To build one of these plans, we would have to either sell or rent our house. It's a two bedroom, older house, and it would need a lot of work to do either. There would have to be moving sales to weed out all our extra stuff that wouldn't fit into a smaller home.

The hardest part is that we would have to change our life style tremendously if we moved to the cabin. In Evansville, we are accustomed to a five minute drive to the grocery store, pharmacy, bank, library, etc. We have both been taking classes from time to time at Ivy Tech Community College. We swim and work out at the YMCA. We have a church that we like. We belong to organizations that we wouldn't be able to attend any more: poetry group, photography group, local authors group, Toastmasters, and the Arts Council. We have friends and family we see regularly who we wouldn't see very much because we would be an hour and 15 minute drive away--going and coming back would be 2 ½ hours total! In the winter we would be driving in the dark after 4:00 pm, and I'm night blind!

What I really would like to do is keep the cabin,

the size it is now, and the house. The house means a lot to me--it is from the days when Shirley was growing up. I know the neighborhood, I love the wildlife and the woods behind us. I love the pond, woodshed, and the raised garden with stones laid in front of it that John built for us with his own hands. John said the 21 years he has lived here with me is the longest he's lived anywhere! I've lived here 45 years. It is home.

But the cabin is the fiber of John and me. It is our dream place; it's what we've both always wanted! We love the woods and the lake. We love the tinkling and singing of Girly Creek. We like the country, the red hills, the wildflowers, and the animals. We planned the cabin together, built it together--it is ours through and through. I would like to spend more time at the cabin!

If we stayed at the cabin more often, fishing, canoeing, and hiking, instead of going to a vacation destination, we could afford to keep it. If we made a place to sleep downstairs by the wood stove when it was cold, it would help. Also, having a shower or a place to bathe would help tremendously--even an outdoor shower. We could build a simple Japanese-type bath behind the cabin with three walls, a plastic shower curtain, and something on which to stand. The person bathing would need a pan of warm water with which to wash and a metal pitcher of warm water to pour over oneself to rinse. The water could be heated on the propane stove, on the wood stove in the winter, or warmed by the sun in the summer.

It would be good to have the cabin in case of an emergency as well. What if our house burned down? There would be a place to live. What if the cities were invaded by some hostile force? There would be an out of the way retreat. What if something happened to the food or water supply? There would be a place to go where there is water (the lake and sometimes Girly Creek), there is firewood (seven acres of trees), and John could hunt in the woods for meat.

We could eat nuts, berries, and other wild edible plants. This is a subject I've been interested in for a long time. A couple of years ago, I made fried dandelion blossoms, and we ate them for supper. They were good.

A long time ago, my neighbor lady told me about poke and eggs. I remember her kitchen was toasty warm as we leaned our elbows on the table her late husband had built. She was telling me how they ate a lot of wild greens back in the Depression.

"My Joe loved poke and eggs," she said. "Pick

poke leaves in early spring when they're tender." I remember her telling me to pour off the water when you're cooking poke--that was very important! She helped me pick the poke that spring--just in case!

Don't eat any wild plants if you aren't sure of what part you can eat and what the full instructions are!

We don't know now what will be our solution, or what we'll end up doing about the cabin. It's a toss-up!

When it was nearly spring, John and I went to the cabin for the day. I had cleaned out our utensil drawer at home and brought the extras to the cabin. Bob came over, and he said that Shelly was in bed with a bad cold. They talked and John told him we were planning to walk over on the other side of the dam by Dry Lake in the Hoosier National Forest. John asked him if he would want to walk with us. He said his foot was bothering him, so he'd better not. He also said that there had been a terrible storm that had knocked down a lot of the trees, covering the four-wheeler trail where we were planning to walk.

After he left we prepared to go. I noticed the

flowers I brought from home, the tall pink phlox and the Easter flowers, were coming up. Down by the creek we saw some spring beauties blooming. Spring was coming, for sure!

It was a gray day. When we arrived at the lake, it was slate-colored. Walking the path back to the spillway, I found a piece of flint that was worked along the edge and had a notch in it. It appears to be useful for cutting and scraping.

We walked across the dam and back into the woods. On our right was a pine forest along the lake. Beautiful.

Bob was right: the four wheeler path was covered over with downed trees. In between the fallen trunks, were thickets of greenbrier. I had been all scratched up by them before, so John showed me how to step on them from the side. I could pass on by without that problem.

"I could use a machete about now for these weeds," John joked.

We hiked up a steep, steep hill--almost a mountain--so we walked through the greenbrier and downed trees slowly.

Finally we found the pond we had seen all those

years ago. It was large, full of water, and lily pads were floating on the water. We could see trails where deer had walked down to get a drink. Walking all around the pond, we had a good view of it. I found a small white feather with a couple of charcoal-colored designs in it. John thought it might be a woodpecker wing feather.

Afterwards, when we started back down, I couldn't see the lake anymore, so I had no idea which way to go. John surveyed it, though.

"If we are lost, we could spend the night under a pile of leaves and be warm as toast," John said. Somehow this didn't sound appealing to me. He found a deer trail. Following it, so we didn't have to walk back through the downed trees, we made good time. We came upon a beautiful rocky creek, shining and moving along, as we were walking beside it. The hill dropped and there were huge slabs of rock down below.

"A bluff may have eroded away leaving those rocks," John suggested. "We can see the creek below it still." I walked quickly up to see the creek circling behind a hill and moving below.

Walking on down, we finally came to another creek. John found a small skull crouched on a rock; he thought it was some kind of a cat skull, or raccoon. Later he looked it up and said it was a raccoon. There were some big blocks of rocks.

Then we saw bottles, cans, a large rusty hinge, and a metal boat seat laying around in between trees.

"We're back to civilization," he said.

We followed a different four-wheeler path--it was low, had a big rut running along it, and was wet. Then we were back to the pine forest, and I could see the lake through the pines. We weren't going to spend the night under a pile of leaves. John, my woodsman, had led us out. All right!

After walking across the dam and the spillway, we decided to walk to the other exit--it had been a long time since we'd walked out that way. Back at the cabin, we quickly packed up the car and headed for a place to eat supper!

On the way to the cabin, John needed to mail a package, so we stopped at the post office in Lynnville, IN. We passed an old garage with a slate roof. Looking around, I saw the grocery store was open. There was also a restaurant, bank, funeral home, and a gas station.

I remembered one time when we came to Lynnville to canoe with Jessica in the lake formed from an old strip mine. It's a beautiful, interesting lake.

Back on the highway, John noticed the trailer being pulled by a truck in front of us didn't have a license plate.

"Citizen's arrest, citizen's arrest!" I said, imitating Barney on the Andy Griffith Show.

"There are three of them!" John said about the number of guys in the truck.

"Never mind," I said. We laughed.

It was not yet spring, but the sun was shining, the sky was blue, and the weather mild. Hawks were sitting in trees, looking for breakfast along the highway.

Later I noticed that the log cabin down the road from our cabin was sold again. We had looked at it a while back, but the logs weren't in very good shape! The For Sale sign was gone and a truck was parked up there by the garage.

Turning into the lane, our driveway, then parking as close to our cabin as we could get, we walked up the steps to unlock the cabin door. John built a fire in the wood stove.

We brought the futon we had just purchased, thinking we would stay at the cabin more often in the winter if we could sleep downstairs by the wood stove.

The futon would be the couch in the daytime and a bed at nighttime, and it wouldn't take up any extra space.

We carried out the Adirondack double chair that we had used for our couch all this time, but now it would be outdoor seating as originally intended. I swept the floor before we carried in the futon frame. After we had it in place, we returned to the truck for the mattress. I never dreamed that it would be a bigger problem than carrying the frame, but it was. For one thing it was big and awkward, and another was that we couldn't get a good grip on it. So John folded it in half, tying a rope around each end, so we could each hold onto the rope.

After we had the futon and mattress in place, we carried in the end table, setting it in place. I had also brought a small end table I had built several years ago--it has a mosaic top (I had used small tiles, flat rocks, broken china, etc.) and the wood was painted with orange shellac. Then I spread a colorful printed throw over the futon, a couple of pillows that coordinated with it, and the braided rug we previously had in front of the couch. It looked good, so we sat on it, hugging the fire, relaxing and talking for a while.

Hunger caught up with us, so we carried in the cooler containing the food that we brought with us.

Deciding to warm the leftover pizza, we wrapped two slices each, in foil. We laid them on top of the wood stove. While they were warming, we strolled down to the steps by Girly Creek.

"I just saw some little fish swimming down the creek!" John said.

"Where?" I asked. We had never seen fish in the creek before.

"I'll try to turn them back down this way so you can see them." He takes off up the creek, but he couldn't find them. We walked along the creek, admiring the bright green ferns along the far side.

"Are ferns always this green in the winter?" I asked.

"I think they are. Here's a deer trail where they walked into the creek!" He pointed to a worn place on the edge of the creek. "Look here. See the deer tracks?" he asked me, pointing to the tracks along the creek.

"Yes, I do. I wonder when the deer were here?"

"Probably when we were inside the cabin."

Remembering the pizza, we ran to the cabin, turning them over on the stove. John needed a few acorns for a project, so we walked up to Oak Flat. Even in the winter it was a beautiful place. The oak trees were spread out, and their leaves were deeply piled on the forest floor. I pushed some leaves back with my foot, searching for acorns.

Green cedar trees circled the area. Walking over to the cedars, I saw several small pine trees growing among the other trees. That made me so happy! We both found a few acorns, so we hurried back to the cabin to eat our pizza.

We wanted to visit Bob and Shelly, so John called to see if they were home. They were, so we took the short cut, crossing the creek. When we were there, telling them about our futon, Shelly wanted to see it, so she and I walked down to our cabin.

She liked the futon, and we sat on it, talking.

"I love your cabin," she said. "It's so great you can live in the city, doing all your activities, but have this place to come to whenever you want."

"Yes. When the world gets to me, and I'm tired of the TV and noise, I want to be out here in this peaceful place," I said.

After a while, we walked back up to their log cabin to join the guys. It was such a pretty day, I couldn't believe it. I love coming to the cabin!